Under The Big Top

Written by Members of The Senior Circus Works

Illustrated by Alison K. Paolini

Edited by Hannie J. Voyles

TRAFFORD

© Copyright 2005 SCW and Hannie J. Voyles & Alison K. Paolini.
All rights reserved. No part of this publication may be reproduced, stored in a retrieval system, or transmitted, in any form or by any means, electronic, mechanical, photocopying, recording, or otherwise, without the written prior permission of the author.

Senior Circus Works is indebted to award-winning author T. E. Watson and his company Book Builders.net, for their technical assistance and the time, energy, and dedication they gave our project.

B/W Illustrations by Alison K. Paolini

Clown Illustration pg 212 Marleen Heeman

Note for Librarians: a cataloguing record for this book that includes Dewey Decimal Classification and US Library of Congress numbers is available from the Library and Archives of Canada. The complete cataloguing record can be obtained from their online database at:
www.collectionscanada.ca/amicus/index-e.html
ISBN 1-4120-4666-1
Printed in Victoria, BC, Canada

TRAFFORD

Offices in Canada, USA, Ireland, UK and Spain
This book was published *on-demand* in cooperation with Trafford Publishing. On-demand publishing is a unique process and service of making a book available for retail sale to the public taking advantage of on-demand manufacturing and Internet marketing. On-demand publishing includes promotions, retail sales, manufacturing, order fulfilment, accounting and collecting royalties on behalf of the author.

Book sales for North America and international:
Trafford Publishing, 6E–2333 Government St.,
Victoria, BC v8t 4p4 CANADA
phone 250 383 6864 (toll-free 1 888 232 4444)
fax 250 383 6804; email to orders@trafford.com

Book sales in Europe:
Trafford Publishing (UK) Ltd., Enterprise House, Wistaston Road Business Centre, Wistaston Road, Crewe, Cheshire cw2 7rp UNITED KINGDOM
phone 01270 251 396 (local rate 0845 230 9601)
facsimile 01270 254 983; orders.uk@trafford.com

Order online at:
www.trafford.com/robots/04-2474.html

10 9 8 7 6 5 4 3 2

Senior Circus Works dedicates
this collection to all the seniors
whose voices we share.

PREFACE

This collection, UNDER THE BIG TOP, began simply enough: Senior citizens in two communities came together and, as they began to write their memories, we learned about their past. We gained insights into the hardships, the laughter, the demands and expectations of those lives. Within these images, we bring the realities of another time - a time that serves as a forerunner of this century that has its own mysteries and perplexities.

We write about treasured memories of growing up in a different and vanished world. We write about family members. We write about our hardships, pain and joy. Even those who no longer function well were able to wrestle some startling memories to the surface. Once we became a group and shared part of our lives, a common commitment emerged: "I am feeling less sad, less lonely, ---- less lost." The act of writing has given us function and purpose again. To find that others had experiences and emotions similar to our own makes each meeting of the Seniors' writing group socially and intellectually stimulating as we validate one another.

It may be said that the death of an old person is like the burning of a library.

We are the ones who can still tell others what it was like, what it meant to have lived through most of the 20th century. We were born in a time when there was no television, no passenger jet, no microwave, computer or super highway. There were only 48 states not 50. Life was slower, harder, and poorer. Or it was better and more idyllic! We write to clear our mental attics! In so doing, we understand our lives and ourselves a little better. This is the legacy for children and grandchildren so that they, in turn, may feel a greater connection. Over time it became clear that collecting our work is of great importance as it captures a century as we lived it, as we knew it. We know that we bring the voice of personal history - not as we learn it from events and dates and places, but from folks who lived every minute and shared their tears through the Great Depression, a time of great poverty, two world wars, a Pearl Harbor, Korea, Vietnam.... With this recognition, the writing groups in two different communities decided to collect and bring the "best" of their works for posterity.

Some 50 senior writers established a process of the collection of some 150 stories and poetry to be read, rated, edited, grouped and formatted for electronic submission. Each selection was read by three raters in the neighboring community by a joint committee. The group held "blind" readings, ranked and scored each entry. They established criteria and offered editing suggestions while maintaining "the lilt of every voice." Out of this process, a theme emerged: Life is often said to be a circus, hence, UNDER THE BIG TOP, full of three ring acts and performances on the high wire; full of false starts and failures, stunts, jugglers, clowns, or a flying trapeze.... We realize that we are like elephants: We lumber along; we have good ears and fantastic memories. Also, like us, elephants don't jump! It is this theme that gave us shape and purpose. It provided a focus that enabled us to organize our material in the "circus" sections that we now bring you: 50 voices that speak of more than 75 years of history.

We will always be indebted to our members who gave so much support to this project, but passed away before we finished.
We include their work posthumously.

Beverly Strisower
Hannie J. Voyles

TABLE OF CONTENTS

I. Enter The Ring

Words . . . . Roger Honzik 11

Grandpa Gullig's Circus . . . . Mary McCartney 12

The Woman Of Years . . . . Alison K. Paolini 16

Yellow Pine, Idaho . . . . Kay Hinerman 18

Rich Little Poor Girl . . . . Karen Romig 22

What I Want My Children and
Grandchildren to Know About Me . . . . Phyllis Wesbecher 25

Where is Jesse James Now? . . . . Sally Wallis 27

My First Job . . . . Kay Hinerman 29

Thanksgiving at The Farm . . . . Delores S. Squyers 31

A Dream Came True . . . . Ann Neilsen 33

Reflection . . . . Roger Honzik 36

A Trip to Remember . . . . Jim Laird 37

Memories of Wash Day . . . . Kay Hinerman 40

My Lost Garden . . . . Delores S. Squyers 42

Aida . . . . Norma Obitz 44

Living Alone Among People . . . . Ellen Eagar 48

The Church of My Childhood . . . . Delores S. Squyers 50

II. Bring On The Clowns

The Black Cat Café . . . . Ariel Edmudson 55

The Book . . . . Norma Obitz 56

Mother's Wisdom . . . . Florence Johanson 60

Rooster Savvy	Kay Hinerman	62
Collector's Item	Dawn McFarland	64
Not In My Watermelon Patch	Lois Adams	65
The Dutiful	Barbara Lang	68
Who Goes First	Bee Mandell	69
Bathtub Beer	Jim Laird	70
Ah, How Well I Don't Remember	Karen Romig	72
My Pleasure	Roger Honzik	75
Splaalaat!	Marion Williams	76
I Cry For My Mother	Florence Johanson	77
The Seduction	Barbara Lang	78
The Pie Crust Lesson	Kay Hinerman	79
Cow College Comedians	Sally Wallis	82
Mister Tip Over	Darlene Fuentes	84
Traffic Tickets	Vesta Steinacker	86
Family Circus Mama Mia! That's Some Spicy Sauce!	Karen Romig	88
Drop Kick	Karen Romig	89
Name That Tuna	Karen Romig	90
Well-Suited	Karen Romig	91

III. Elephants On Parade

The Perfect Wedding	Bee Mandell	93
To Begin Again	Ariel Edmundson	95
First Love	Karen Romig	96
If Only	Roger Honzik	99
Metaphorically Speaking	Alison K. Paolini	100
Missouri Day In Fowler, Colorado	Vesta Steinacker	101

Remembered .... Roger Honzik 103
Why I Ride A Motorcycle .... Ellen Eagar 104
Moments .... Roger Honzik 105
Love Then, Love Now .... Alison K. Paolini 106
Welcome to Ethiopia .... Carmen Jury 107
Evening Themes .... Roger Honzik 109
The Ear Piercing .... Kay Hinerman 110
A Narrow Escape .... Carol Jean Main 112
Boarding School Days .... Barbara Lang 115
Why I Never Learned to Type .... Phyllis Wesbecher 119
The World Turns in Five Minute Segments D. McFarland 120

IV. Walking the Tightrope

The Window .... Hannie J. Voyles 125
Our Miracle Trip - V. E. Day 1995 ... Florence Johanson 126
I Saw Bob Hope .... Jim Laird 130
On the Brink 1 .... Zigrid Vidners 132
On the Brink II .... Zigrid Vidners 135
P.J. On the Rifle Range .... Jim Laird 140
Well .... Roger Honzik 142
A Desperate Prayer Answered .... Frank H. Stagner 144
War Comes to Our Town .... Laszlo Daroczi 150
We Are All in it Together .... Luther Mandell 155
Preparing The Way .... Dawn McFarland 156
Storm on The Moon .... Ariel Edmundson 159
The Day I Ate Orange Guck .... Roger Honzik 160

Glenn Comes Home .... Barbara Lang 162
Coming of Age .... Laszlo Daroczi 166

V. Sideshow Wonders

Sunday Morning .... Richard Cory 170
Hey to That City by The Bay .... Ariel Edmundson 172
Miss Garrett .... Florence Johanson 173
Magic Night .... Ariel Edmundson 175
All You Can Carry For a Buck .... Richard Cory 176
Audition At The Wintergarden .... Alison K. Paolini 178
Kelly .... Norma Obitz 180
Brandy's Rabbit .... Jim Laird 184
Escapade .... Ariel Edmundson 186
Burnt Toast .... Luther Mandell 187
Early Morning Light .... Carol Jean Main 188
Jury Duty .... Dick Cory 189
Sifting .... Roger Honzik 191
Remembering and Wondering Why? .. Richard A. Main 192
Snow ... Maybe .... Alison K. Paolini 196
The Veil .... Delores S. Squyers 195
Death Stalked the Kern .... Carol Jean Main 198
Awareness! .... Carol Jean Main 204
The East End of Night .... Roger Honzik 205
In Retrospect .... Dawn McFarland 206
The Vase .... Beverly Strisower 207
A Little Birds Tale .... Beverly Strisower 209
Acknowledgements 213

I.
Enter The Ring

Voices of Truth

Words convey such beauty and grace, yet they can be wild and inspire love and so much more. In time words will cradle us with peace as we become one with them.

Words

Roger E. Honzik

I find a warming truth among the words I read. People write from their hearts or minds as they need. The writer's need often comes from the reader, who asks to be soothed, surprised or loved. At times the reader melts with guilt, pity or joy. Words make flowers grow and love and friendship bloom. Writers sense the voids in life and weave new pathways to dream.

The poet writes from a different place. He takes the feelings from those around and puts them on, as though sackcloth, to better understand the needs and dreams of those who search. His eyes magnify the truth of the words we have to read and hold.   Oh! But then we listeners are the key. Words, simple little words move mountains, and so much more. Words change hearts. Think of some of the words and thoughts most of us heard together in our class.

In some of our stories we were reminded of the beauty as well as the harshness of life. Think back to the Russian soldiers who shot down the grandfather while his little grandson could only watch without understanding the brutality of war. --- What yoke of sadness did we bear with the ageing widow who was struggling to move past the grief of losing her mate. She saw the color of her husbands eyes reflected in the wild flowers growing on the hills they once strolled. --- What soul could ever forget the horror of the images that will ever haunt the young Dutch girl who was stripped of family, friends and countrymen by that godless hoard who meant to destroy a whole nation of people. How deep the knife of sadness cuts, how lasting are its scars. --- Recall the touching anxious steps of searching, year upon year, as a sister sought her siblings. How time and space seemed to snatch them away forever, yet each was found by careful and persistent searching. The last of the family to be found had only a cold stone marker to show his place of his final rest. Did you not feel the-stoneshetouched as she quietly said her last goodbyes?

The comfort, understanding and care expressed in simple words draws us together to share our humanity.

Grandpa Gullig's Circus

Mary McCartney

I loved to sit on Grandma's lap in her old wooden rocking chair. She would feed me homemade bread; butter and sugar, with all the crust cut off and cut into little pieces. I would sit there quietly while she told me stories about Grandpa Gullig's Circus.

I never got to meet Grandpa, because he died eight years before I was born. Grandma would tell me about his life, his circus and the many memories stored in his big circus trunk. What great stories were to spill from that ornamented treasure chest in Grandma's bedroom?

Grandpa Andrew Gullig was born in 1848 in Fon du Lac, Wisconsin. He was a thin and wiry man, under six feet tall. He was the eleventh child in a large German family.

As a young man, he lived near Baraboo, Wisconsin where the American Circus began in nearby Charles, Illinois. It was the traditional wintering spot for the circus.

Grandpa was only fifteen when he got a job cleaning the animal cages of the circus. He liked working with the animals, but his real love was the high wire acts. Night after night he enviously watch the man on the flying trapeze, learning and hoping for the day he would dare to walk the wire.

By the time he was thirty years old, in 1878, he had traveled all over the world. During a stop in Brazil, he adopted a poor little, five-year-old orphan boy. The Brazilian circus master had trained the child to walk the tight rope by in-humane methods. The ringmaster started training him on thick wires when he was barely able to walk. The child's bare little toes struggled to grasp the wire. Every time he fell from the wire to the ground, the circus master would beat him with a switch or burn him on his bottom with his ever-present cigar.

As the boy grew older, the wire size was reduced and the height was increased, but he still had nothing to cover his raw feet and the switching continued. Grandpa's heart went out to this poor urchin as he watched the ringmaster force the boy to scale the eight-foot high wire. The boy had, by now, become an accomplished tight rope walker. Somehow, Grandpa was able to adopt Juan to come to America with him. One time, Grandma let me hold the little Brazilian boy's adoption papers. The papers were in a foreign language, so she couldn't read them.

Little Juan became a featured performer in the circus. He would also do high wire acts across gorges and other breathtaking acts. He was eye catching in his bright yellow tights and his green open-vested variegated shirt with puffy, red sleeves. He was always careful to not show his scars and never removed his shirt or pants where anyone could see them. The only person he trusted was Grandpa.

Grandpa bought half interest in the Bridges circus. Mr. & Mrs. Bridges were lion tamers and older than Grandpa. They were glad to have a pardoner to help them. Like most circus performers, confidence played a big role in creating the spectacle of daring skill the audience paid to see. Mr. Bridges had suffered a number of close calls with the lions. He had been pawed and one time the lion had mauled him. One day he became overly confident and turned his back on the lion after it refused to jump through a fire ring and the lion mauled Mr. Bridges to death. The tumbling fire ring caught the straw in the tent on fire, sending animals and people scattering. By some miracle, the volunteer firefighters were at ringside, showing off their horse-driven water pump wagon and quickly put the fire out. The town constable was there and he shot and killed the lion.

Knowing "the show must go on" the widow Bridges and Grandpa now worked together. In the evening, after the show, they would go in the office and count the day's receipts.

In those days, it was not proper for an un-chaperoned man and a woman to be in one and others company. Grandpa, being a man of integrity and for appearance sake, married the widow.

Twelve years later, another tragic accident occurred. His wife was feeding the lions, later than usual and the hungry, unruly lions attacked and killed her. Overcome with his losses and tired of the constant travel, Grandpa sold the circus to Barnum and Bailey.

Grandpa bought a farm in Marion, Illinois. He settled down to a calmer life as a farmer. Soon he met Julia Blanchard who worked at the Elgin Watch factory. Grandpa was in love for the first time. He was fifty-five at this time and Julia was forty-five. Grandpa loved kids, but in those days he thought they were too old to have a family.

In time, Julia wanted someone in the house to take some of the workload from her. When the opportunity presented itself in 1910, they took in a three year old girl, Gracie Mae, who became my mother in 1934.

Grandma told me all these wonderful stories about Grandpa Gullig and now I was anxious to see what was in his circus trunk. She opened the pretty arched lid so I could discover all the treasures that Grandpa had saved. We found posters from all the world where he had gone and pictures of growling lions, pretty girls standing on the backs of elephants and Grandpa on the high wire.

We found his costumes of dark colored tights and long sleeved jersey shirts. Over these Grandpa worn multi colored sequined shorts and a bolero jacket of sequins. We found four colorful caps and two top hats. Down in the very bottom I spied a little red box. Inside was money, but we could not spend it for candy because it was from other around the world. Grandma let me keep the box to put pennies in.

We found a big pocket watch in a velvet pouch. It had a long chain and was real shiny. Grandma ran her hand around the edge of the watch and the lid popped open. Inside was some writing on a ten-dollar bill and Grandma read it and it said, "Andrew you are right. Our ten year marriage has been good and profitable. You won the bet. It was the right thing to do."

On the other side at the bottom of the trunk was a small pile of letters tied with a blue ribbon. I noticed that every time Grandma looked in the trunk, she would push the letters out of the way. One day Grandma was standing, leaning on one crutch and stirring a pot of baked beans on top of her tall, wood-heating stove. When her back was to me, I grabbed the letters out of the trunk.

I ask Grandma to tell me another story about the trunk. She said that was all. Just then I pulled the letters out of my pocket and said, "Grandma, you forgot these." She sat down in her rocker and sighed, "Child, I'm not sure we should read Papa's private letter's?" I begged, "Please Grandma."

The first letter dated June 9,1879:

Papa! I am happy to be your son. The cook is teaching me to read and write English. I hope you are proud of me. Your son, Juan

July 8, 1879:

Papa, thank you for giving me a birthday present. July 7 is going to be my birthday from now on. The cook said she enjoyed making my birthday cake. I never ate cake before but I really liked it. Love,

Your son, Juan.

August 20, 1879

Papa, I'm so happy. How can I be so lucky that you love me and made me your son? I love you Papa. I don't understand why you have given me so much, my life, your love. But, Papa, you don't have to pay me for doing the high wire. I was surprised that you have been putting money away for me from the first day. Love, your son, Juan.

I looked at Grandma's face. She had tears in her eyes. Then, swiftly, she picked up the last letter. It was different than the others. The letter was bigger and it felt real nice. Grandma unfolded the official looking letter and read:

Mr. Andrew Gullig: You and your famous Gullig and Bridges Circus are invited to a command performance on Buckingham Palace Green, the 25th day of August, year of our Lord, 1880. Sir Neel de Aubigey will handle all the arrangements and supply all your needs for the performance. I, Queen Victoria, set my hand to this invitation and will welcome you at 2:00 P.M., August 25,1880.

Grandma kissed me on the top of the head, brushed the hair out of my eyes and said, "Child, I'm glad we read the letters. All this time I thought they were love letters.

"But Grandma, they were!"

I have met women, who in retirement had taken up the paintbrush, and without expecting much the results surprised them and the women were reborn.

The Woman Of Years

Alison K. Paolini

Painting her heart out
The woman of years
Expresses pent up emotions.
Shades of red and hues of blue.
Her palette never ends nor does it falter.
Color flows to canvas or paper, and
She releases her thoughts.
Her attitude comes through with
Brush strokes, strong or smooth.
Quick, or slow and sultry, halting or even.
Perhaps she paints a flower,
Pansy, petunia or poinsettia.
Maybe a glorious iris or a simple daisy.
But.. Look.. She has given it life!
Her life is richer, her eyes softer.
Heart beat, blood pressure, relaxed.
I see this, I live this, I declare this.
She never marked a canvas with color.
She never spent time with pencil, pen or brush.
The day came. The desire arose..
She noted and searched ... and found ...
Other women on the same quest.
Together they learned, created, rejoiced.
Together they, all women of years,
Grew into themselves and ripened.
The years were enriched by the art,
By the friendships and by the newness.

The brain was at work, the hands made to follow.
She who thought she had stopped learning,
Now was delving into age-old information.
But to her, it was fresh.
She looked at everything with fresh eyes...
She saw colors, always there, but never seen.
She mixed colors and painted what she saw.
Being a woman of years she understood,
She welcomed with open arms
She celebrated her new life.

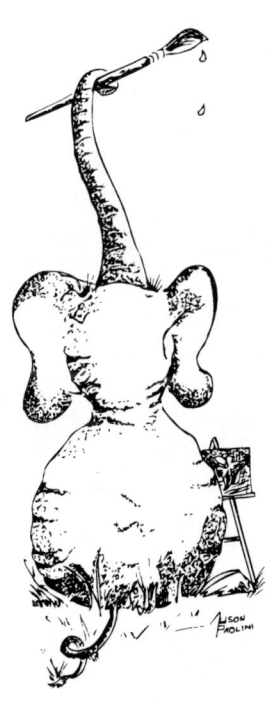

Yellow Pine, Idaho, was an example of the pack stations and mining towns along the Salmon River and its tributaries from the 1960's to the 80's. I now realize how fortunate our family was to sample the "everyday life" in these places.

Yellow Pine, Idaho

Kay Hinerman

From 1960 to 1975 our family spent two weeks every summer camping and fishing on Johnson Creek. The name was not synonymous of its name. It was a meandering medium-sized stream comparable to the West Branch of the Feather River in places. This river-sized creek emptied into the East Fork of the South Fork of the Salmon River in central Idaho. Johnson Creek boasted wonderful limits of native Rainbow Trout and Salmon. Originally we went for the fishing; but that changed with time as we learned about Yellow Pine.

There were two main roads that lead to Yellow Pine. A one and a half lane dirt road 50 miles from Mc Call, Idaho, was one way to Yellow Pine. It was not advisable to take this road if one was pulling a trailer. Often travelers had to stop, move rocks and clear branches to pass. The road was very rough and filled with large potholes. One could depend on meeting one or two logging trucks along the way as well. This was a challenge as the traveler going toward the river was always on the drop-off side. It was not unusual to have a wheel hanging over the cliff as you gunned the engine and lumbered by.

The second route was 75 miles from Cascade, a small town 20 miles south of Mc Call. It was paved for 20 miles, and the unpaved part was not so rough. It was maintained well for an unpaved road as it led past the ranger station and Cox Guest Ranch, which was a working dude ranch during those years. Regardless of the chosen road, after five minutes of driving, the wilderness area became very evident. The hamlet of Yellow Pine lies where Johnson Creek Road meets the road that leads past the East Fork of the South Fork. The dirt road broadens into about one city block.

There were three commercial buildings in the town, and four

businesses. On the left the first business was a shed-like building that housed the garage where automotive repairs were made. Next, were two businesses, actually, run by two families in one building. The left side of the building was the general store. There, a complete grocery store existed if you could push the fishing tackle, lures, bait and other paraphernalia aside. There, a skeleton inventory of most grocery items camping tourists might need and want existed. Two floor to ceiling refrigerators contained fresh milk, eggs, butter, bacon, beer and pop. The large chest freezer held a selection of frozen meat, vegetables and ice cream. The freezer supplied the meat and other perishable vittles needed for the restaurant menu. A very lucky fisherman could also have his "catch" frozen and kept till he was ready to pack up and move on.

In addition, one corner boasted a full service post office, postcards and souvenirs. Liquor, beer and wine were also for sale. A book exchange of pocket and hardcover books was displayed in the post office area. The back of the store was the living quarters for one of the families who ran the store.

The bar could be accessed through a front door, or the door that never closed from grocery store side. This room was about twice the size of the grocery store.

The bar along one side of the room was nothing short of unique. After the tourists left by November, the six adults and seven children who were permanent residents, worked for three winters on the completion of the bar. The vertical part of the bar was wood paneled, but the top was a work of art. Small pieces of different kinds of prominently grained wood indicative to the area had been sanded, varnished and set together with a first class wood glue into a mosaic. The entire bar had then been lacquered so it was impervious to any moisture.

Short orders as well as complete meals were served over the bar or on the six tables placed on the well waxed and oiled pine floor. The table area doubled as a dance floor and a stage at one end was roomy for the many guest musicians and bands that found their way into Yellow Pine on weekends. Food that required an oven was prepared in the kitchen of the living quarters. There was no lack of alcoholic and soft drinks. If patrons wanted to dance, the tables and chairs were pushed aside. A jukebox of tunes furnished the music.

Across the street from the grocery store/bar was the Yellow Pine Hotel. This establishment had four bedrooms, one bathroom and a bar, meals had to be purchased at the bar across the street. The hotel doubled as a pack station for hunters who went elk hunting in early November. Corrals behind the hotel were used for the horses that were trucked into Yellow Pine each fall for hunting.

The link between Yellow Pine and the outside world was a single-engine Cessna plane that carried the mail and supplies in and out twice a week. On occasion, it had to be called to make unscheduled trips for medical emergencies.

This was quite a complicated process. The Mc Call airport was called from the crank wall phone in the store. Everyone hoped the plane was on the ground and available to make the run. The airport would give an estimated time the plane would leave. That time never included the airtime to Cox's Guest Ranch where the one and only airstrip lay. Flight time was about 15 minutes. The canyon walls surrounding the airstrip were 2,500 to 3,000 feet straight up, and in order to land, the pilot had to fly toward the opposite canyon wall, swerve and "switch back" to the opposite side. Thus, he gently descended. Take off required quite a few more "switch backs" as the ascension was more difficult. If someone had to go to the hospital, there was a wild 6-mile ride from the Yellow Pine General Store to the airstrip.

This all became very real one summer day. Georgia, the wife of the grocery store merchant had to make an unscheduled trip. Georgia was 8 ½ months pregnant with their third child. Labor pains started, and her frantic husband called the airport. He nearly forgot to tell them to send a nurse in case the delivery came in flight. Finally the bartender (driving) and Georgia's husband, trying to comfort her arrived at the airstrip. The plane was trying to land, but the pilot was making more than the usual passes due to breezy down drafts. Finally down, a nurse and the pilot jumped out of the plane, loaded Georgia aboard and off they went. This was on a Thursday. The next morning we learned Georgia had given birth to a little girl, joining six year-old twin brothers. On Saturday, the plane returned with Georgia and the baby. We learned she did make it to the hospital in time, but it was a bit dicey for a while.

Yellow Pine is still the Gateway to Idaho's Primitive Area. The years we were part of the summer community it was a wild and friendly town; but today those years are a lost era as time has moved on and progress has moved in.

This is an object lesson for myself and for my children and grandchildren of the pleasure small things can bring. One can be very wealthy on very little; it's a state of mind!

Rich Little Poor Girl

Karen Romig

One evening years ago, when I was all grown up and had a family of my own, my mother and I were reminiscing about my childhood. Suddenly she asked, "Did you mind terribly being poor?" I was stunned. "Poor?" I repeated, wondering what on earth she was talking about. "What do you mean, 'poor'?

We were never POOR! I searched my memory for clues to substantiate my mother's insinuation. There weren't any. I remembered my fifth birthday party, when we had cake and balloons and I got a large red, white and blue ball with stars and stripes on it, and a pair of roller skates from my grandma. I thought of Christmas, when Santa brought me a baby doll complete with crib and layette. I must have misunderstood her; maybe she was confusing my childhood with her own; I knew, however, that she hadn't been poor during her early years either.

"What do you mean, 'poor"?" I repeated, half afraid of the answer. "I had everything I ever wanted-I don't know how you can say that!" I stated defensively, as though she had accused me of a crime. "What are you talking about, for Heaven's sake?" I almost shouted.

"Well, of course you know" she went on, "that when the depression hit, the bottom fell out of your dad's business. He was too proud to take charity or go on relief like so many of our friends did, so we lived on hope and credit."

"Before the crash," she continued, "money was coming in and living was easy. Your dad was a good provider and a social animal. We were constantly invited to parties and he was often the main source of entertainment. Your dad could sing and play the trumpet and tell wonderful stories in a dozen different dialects. He could quote Omar Khayam and Shakespeare or launch into Robert Service's "Shooting of Dan McGrew" or "Cremation of Sam McGee", and send shivers down our spines. He could draw caricatures and do magic tricks - make nickels appear in someone's ear or cause a card to disappear with a flick of his wrist" she trailed off in a mist of remembrance I KNEW all this: what I didn't know was that we were poor!

My dad had graduated with a Chemical Engineering degree, but had decided early on that laboratory life was too confining for him, so he became a New York Life insurance agent, much more to his liking. He was good at it, too, and they were living high off the hog until shortly after I was born. Then people became much more interested in the source of their next meal than they were in making premium payments.

I knew nothing of this. We had a house and a car and food on the table and sometimes we went to the movies. Once in awhile we bought Popsicles or ice cream cones. There were often strange men, I remember, sitting on our back step eating a plateful of whatever my mother had in the house. If we were feeding strangers, we must have been rich! And they brought home a brand new baby when I was about five and a half. He came equipped with TWO carriages, a ton of clothes, dozens of bottles, and diapers to burn. If they had money to fritter away on another kid that they really didn't need when they had me, they couldn't have been in much financial trouble...So, where was she coming from?

There was more. "Do you remember Kladeezee clothes?" Mother asked. I did. They had these nifty metal buckle affairs on built-in belts. I had a dark green playsuit that I adored. My brother, Clark, was entranced with the catalog. He always wanted whatever the kid holding the neatest toy was modeling. He never understood that the boat or car or airplane didn't come with the outfit. "I sold that line to my friends" she explained, "so I could buy them at a discount for you two. Besides that, " she went on, " I begged the school principal, who was a family friend, to give me as many substitute teaching jobs as he could wangle. That bought us gas money and put food on the table until your dad got a job at Oliver."

Oliver Iron Mining Company was a major employer in the Itasca Iron Range of northern Minnesota. My dad managed to get a job in the office. I'm sure it was a great relief for my mother to have steady money coming in, but it must have been a desperation move for Daddy and a bitter pill to swallow. Whatever the case, he never let on to me that this wasn't just what he wanted to do. I was entranced with the big, bumpy-top lunchbox he toted to work in the morning. It was, I thought, like having a little picnic lunch every day - what fun!

"Well, so," I countered, taking this all in, "you were working two jobs and so was Daddy, if you count the little bit of insurance business he was doing. Everything was cheap and everybody was hurting. It sounds to me" I went on, "as though you were pretty well-fixed, by comparison. Where does the "poor" come in?"

"It comes in" she replied, because of the fact that if your dad had a nickel, he'd spend a dime and treat all his friends. And if he didn't have it, he'd borrow it. The buddies who had been so quick to down a drink or dinner during your dad's salad days were now pressing for payment for loans they had extended when the nickels ran out. So most of what the two of us took in", she continued, "went right out again in somebody else's pocket."

The conversation then took a slightly different tack. Your dad ran for public office", she went on with a wistful smile, "and you were his campaign chairman. Whenever you two went for a walk downtown, you'd advise everybody you met to "Vote for my daddy!" "He lost the election by a very narrow margin". Mother hesitated, then went on somewhat conspiratorially, "I was really rather glad he didn't win", she confided, "I'm sure it would have meant endless rounds of drinks and poker games with the "good ol' boys" - probably more than the probate judge position paid - and that would have been total disaster for our already decimated budget.

I was beginning to get the picture, but so was Mother. As I started to say, "I guess you're right -- we really were poor", she offered, "You know, all things considered, we were pretty well off at that! It's just too bad it has taken me so long to realize just how rich we really were!"

During the Great Depression a lively imagination was necessary for children to entertain themselves during play. Today with battery-operated toys and computers a child is robbed of depending on their creativity for playtime.

What I Want My Children and Grandchildren to Know About Me

*Phyllis Wesbecher
(d. April 2003)*

When I was very small, the country was going through a depression. Large numbers of people were out of work; almost every day someone would knock on our door asking for something to eat. We didn't have much, but my mother never turned anyone away who was hungry.

We had very few toys compared to what children have today. We played a lot of make-believe games. My best girlfriend lived next door. She and I pretended we were dressed beautifully. We would look for rocks on our graveled roads. Most of the roads were graveled; only a few main streets were paved. The rocks we picked represented our cosmetics. I found a long, narrow rock that was my lipstick. The round rocks were our powder and rouge. We would describe to each other what we were wearing and we were dressed "fit to kill." This was all make believe.

I also loved paper dolls. I would save pop bottles and turn them in at the store. With fifteen cents I could buy some nice paper dolls. I also had a dollhouse that my brother made for me. He took two orange crates and put one on top of the other. That made four rooms. We tore pages out of an old wallpaper catalog and pasted them on the inside walls of the orange crates. For Christmas I received a tiny couch, a little rocking chair, a table with four chairs and two tiny dolls. My brother made a little Victrola out of a block of wood and he pounded a nail on top. He made records out of cardboard and put a hole in the middle of the round cardboard discs so I could put them on the Victrola. He also made a tiny doll bed. With scraps of material I made covers and pillows for the bed. I think I had so much fun with that dollhouse as little girls nowadays have with their elaborate manufactured dollhouses and furniture.

We didn't need a battery-run stove and appliances like they have now. We used tin cans and some cracked cups and dishes that our mothers didn't use anymore. We made mud pies and cakes and set them on a board in the sun. That was our oven. When the mud dried our cakes and pies were done. Once I made a mud cake and decorated it with Red Hots and gumdrops. It looked so good I took a bite. To my dismay, I had a mouth full of mud!

I see children nowadays with so many toys; they don't know what to play with. Some parents think they have to get their children every new toy or the latest fad that comes out. Most toys run on batteries and children need no imagination.

I realize that children can use computers and are very smart about electronic devices that are rather Greek to me. Times have changed so much from one extreme to another. Although I am not involved in the new electronic age, I wonder if our children today are too involved. Are they missing out on more immediate use of their imagination?

Many farmers in the plain states proudly claimed they allowed Jesse James and his gang to sleep in their barns in the eighteen seventies and eighties. He was a hero then and still is. I decided to write about this and went to the Internet and found six thousand articles about Jesse's life. So, here's the rest of the story.

Where is Jesse James Now?

By Sally Wallis

I hearken back to my childhood when I saw the movie about Jesse James, the famous bank robber. Tyron Power was Jesse and what young girl wasn't in love with him? Equally adored was Henry Fonda who played his brother Frank. The movie describes Jesse and Frank's attempts to avenge their widowed, Mother's death. A vicious railroad company confiscated their farm in Kearney, Missouri to build a railroad to the west and they shot Mrs. James in the head.

Needless to say, these fine boys turned to crime and began robbing trains. They soon shared hero statues in America as our version Robin Hood. Wanted posters sprang up all throughout the United States. The James gang finally disbanded and decided to go straight. In 1882 Bob Ford, a former gang member came to visit Jesse and as he stood on a chair, hanging a picture, Bob Ford shot him in the back. Jesse was still handsome when they buried him in Kearney Missouri.

Not unlike Elvis, folks spotted Jesse for years and swore he was not really dead. In my devotion to him, I searched the faces of every young man I saw, hoping to discover Jesse. It never crossed my mind that since he was born in1847, he would be 96 years old.

To begin my inspired work, I went to the Internet and to my deep chagrin, I found that Jesse's father was alive when Jesse formed his gang. He was a Baptist Minister who helped start William Jewel College in Liberty, Missouri. He died in 1894 while gold mining in California. Their mother married two more times and died peacefully at age ninety. Jesse and Frank began their criminal life after they learned to fight in the Civil war. They roamed the plain states robbing trains and banks.

In 1995, a group of scientist decided to dig up Jesse and test his DNA. They wanted to finalize arguments that Jesse was buried in various other places.

A boy in my High School always claimed to be Jesse's great nephew and with Bobby's wild lifestyle, we thought that was entirely possible. He claimed he had traced his bloodlines and discovered that his great grandmother was Jesse's sister, Susan.

Bobby read that research was underway to find relatives of the famous outlaw, so he contacted the scientists to tell them of his belief that he was a direct relative. They ask Bobby to come to Missouri and allow them to do blood tests to confirm their suspicions. To everyone's delight, it was 99.9% positive that indeed, the outlaw was Bobby's great uncle and that Jesse was buried in the grave in Kearney, Missouri.

The happy ending to my story is that Bobby was invited to come to London and meet the Queen at the opening of a science museum displaying the scientific proof of the value of DNA.

Jobs for kids were hard to come by in 1947. I got my first lesson in economics that spring picking strawberries for the local truck garden farmer.

My First Job

Kay Hinerman

"You better go down to Matsamoto's and fill out an application. Bill said Richard Matsamoto told him at baseball practice Yoshie has arrived from Seattle, and berry picking will start in a week!"

That was the phone conversation with my best friend, Sally. Bill was her high school age brother, and he "knew everything" as far as I was concerned. On Saturday I rode my bike down Matsamoto's lane to their farm and filled out an application.

"Have you had any experience picking berries, Kay?"

"No," was my reply.

"Well, I have to give first choice to the kids that picked for us last year, but usually not everyone returns, so then I fill the spots with kids who have no experience." "Oh, good, you have your phone number on here, so I can call you if I need you. Thanks for coming by."

It was May 1947, and I was finishing the 7th grade. There was only fieldwork to do in our small community. The Japanese truck farmers had a huge strawberry business and they hired girls 12 years old and older to pick strawberries for them. One of their older daughters came from Seattle to hire, fire, and supervise the berry pickers, as Mr. and Mrs. Matsamoto weren't fluent in English. This year it was Yoshie.

I remember what a long week it was. After school I hardly wanted to leave the house for fear the phone would ring for me and I would miss it. It never occurred to me my folks would call me to the phone, I guess. By Friday night I was beside myself. Would I get to work this year? I'll call Sally.

"Hi, did you get a call to start picking strawberries yet?"

"Oh, yeah, Yoshie called about an hour ago."

"OK, good-bye, I'm getting off the phone so she can get through if she calls me."

29

No call. Saturday morning. Still no call. Sunday morning. No call. I've given up! Sunday night the phone rings. "Hello, Kay, it's Yoshie Matsamoto. Can you come to work tomorrow afternoon?"
"Oh yes, what time?"
"Be here at 4 o'clock. We'll meet on the side lawn, and I'll give everyone her instructions. Be sure to wear jeans, a long-sleeved shirt, and a wide brimmed straw hat. There will be about two hours of hot sun. Also, bring a jug of water. We'll pick till 8 p.m."
"I'll be there. Thanks."
I'm walking on air. Oh, wow. Let's see, five cents a berry cup, eight cups to a carrier. . ." I was carried away with how much money I was going to make. I calculated, and planned how I would spend my earnings. I'd buy all my school clothes . . .on and on I dreamed. The end of Monday's shift dashed those dreams. I'd made $2.00 for 5 carriers. "Oh, this is hard work!" The returnees were picking and not talking, maybe that was the secret. There were lots of things to remember: don't pull the stems off the berries. They aren't fit to ship without stems. Don't throw berries. My rule was don't eat the berries. I found it really slowed down the picking. I did get somewhat faster. That year the season lasted 4 weeks, and at the end of the season I had $28.00.
Yoshie gave us a picnic on the last day. It was the Matsamoto's "thank you" to all of us.

    I picked berries for two more seasons, and I earned $40 the last season. It seemed like a lot of money. I bought a used portable typewriter and had $5 left over! What an accomplishment!

I was 18 years old in November. This was to be my first Thanksgiving in California. When I asked, "What are we bringing to church for Thanksgiving dinner?" I was met with a blank stare. What was I talking about? Thanksgiving here was not spent at church!

Thanksgiving at The Farm

Delores Swenson Squyres

We lived five miles from the church, and Thanksgiving came during the muddy or snowy weather. Anyway, early in November, every family received the list of foods that they were to bring to the dinner. Six items, large servings of each. They wanted to be certain that everyone at the church had all they wanted to eat! Usually, the turkeys were roasted in the church kitchen, in the basement. The cook stoves in that kitchen had large ovens, which looked huge to me, as a child! It was adjacent to the large meeting room, where the meal would be served. The meeting room tables were fairly long, with an aisle between them and space at each end for serving. There were benches on either side of each table for seating. There were some decorations on the table.

Thanksgiving Day arrived. The foods were all prepared and packed up and ready to be transported to the church. We were all excited, looking forward to that special, delicious dinner!

Some years we came in the carriage or wagon, depending on the weather. If it was nice enough weather, the carriage was used. If it was muddy, then it was the wagon we arrived in. The most fun was when there was snow! Then we would have sleigh bells on the horses, and ride in the sled on the fragrant hay. All snuggled up in the blankets and bear rugs, with our heads peeking out, enjoying the clear, frosty air. If it rained, we had oilcloths over us all. It was always a joyous trip, in any weather!

We would arrive at the church, the food would be taken to the kitchen, and my grandfather would put the horses in the barn. We would go into the vestibule and remove coats and overshoes, hats or caps and gloves or mittens, and then we would wait for my grandfather to join us. When he did, we would go in to the church. The fragrance of the turkeys being roasted drifted up to us. How good the church smelled! The church service was held, thanking God for all the blessings he had bestowed upon us during the previous year. There was also a routine part to the service.

After it was completed, we would all go to the basement to eat, by way of the indoor stairs. There wasn't enough space or tables for everyone to eat at once, so there would be a first seating--those who got there first, then a second, and then a third. In the church, we usually sat about the second row from the front, on the right side. On this day, we'd be with the middle group, at the second seating. It was difficult for us children to wait our turn! My grandparents would assure us that there was plenty of food for everyone-all each of us wanted! Those who were waiting stood around the walls of the room, watching those who were eating, and visiting with each other. Children stayed with their families. When they finished eating and the tables were cleared, it was our turn to sit down and enjoy the meal.

It was not the turkey I was excited about. I loved "ost kaka ", a Swedish dish. It was sort of like custard, but it had little holes in it. It was smooth tasting, and to me, it was the best part of the entire dinner! In America, the words meant cheesecake; only it wasn't anything like our cheesecake of today. It was a baked food, made in a round casserole, as a side dish, not a dessert. I ate as much of it as my grandfather would allow. It's all I would have eaten otherwise.

There would be turkey and dressing, gravy, potatoes--mashed ones and scalloped ones, vegetables of various kinds, cranberries, quite a few Swedish foods including the "ost kaka", various kinds of pickles and condiments, and about everything we have now. There would be pumpkin pie with real whipped cream! There were other kinds of pies and cakes for those who wanted them. We all ate until we were absolutely full! There was water to drink, and lots of coffee with cream and sugar.

After the third seating, it was cleanup time and different ones took their turns doing that. Because we lived far away and couldn't stay late, we always helped with what we could. We would leave before it was all completed, because we had such a long trip home, and the chores at home had to be done. But it had been such a glorious and wonderful day! Just thinking about it now fills me with great happiness! Thank you, God! Thanksgiving was one of the joys of my childhood!

Does anybody outgrow the pleasure in toys? Maybe the toys just get more sophisticated!

A Dream Came True

Ann Nielsen

My parents were pretty well off, financially. And thus was their life style, which was void of children. I was an only child for the first eight years of my life and a child to be seen and not heard. A child too often to be left with a sitter when my parents went on vacations. I was blessed to occasionally be part of a family that I wished were my own. They were distant friends of my parents, a family I idolized. Their two daughters had everything that I didn't have, piano lessons, ice-skating lessons and their family car that was a Model A Ford in the year of 1946. That was only a sixteen-year-old car. But, I was fascinated with it, the seat in the rear, called a rumble seat that was in the place of a trunk. It was enough space for three kids or two adults to sit. The horn was no ordinary horn that honked. This one went, ah-ooga, that was personality! As for the color, it was something dark and maybe not even shinny. There was just something about the shape that said it was a real car. Funny how a kid will see things like that.

One time the family invited me to go for a weekend with them to the grandparents of the two girls. I took my little duffel bag with my clothes in it to school on Friday and from school they would be picking me up and taking me via the Model A Ford, all the way from

Long Beach to Ontario, California.

Never did a day move so slowly. I had told some school friends about my adventure and was so excited to see that Model A Ford pull up in front of my school, just for me! That day, I felt I was the luckiest kid ever. Probably this was no big deal to many kids but to me, it was one of the most exciting days of my life. I was going to ride in the rumble seat! I was told that it would be windy and maybe get cold before we reached the grandparents' citrus ranch. We had to be ready to grab hold of the body of the car in front of us or be bounced up off the seat when we hit a bump in the road, being that the rumble seat sits right above the rear wheels. It was windy and it did get cold, but no complaint escaped my lips. I loved the feeling of the wind in my face. A blanket was offered and we three girls to huddle together against the cold after the sun set.

The ranch was a great place to run and play hide and seek, and there was even a swimming pool. I wanted that week- end to last forever!

This was the beginning. Before too long, I gather cardboard boxes, and a knife from the kitchen and lots of Scotch Tape, I made the body of the ideal car, complete with rumble seat. This all fit on my wagon with the tongue of the wagon inside the car to steer while my wagon was pulled by a neighbor kid's bicycle with the promise of equal time driving my car with me pulling the wagon behind the bicycle. What a treasure, for a child!

Fifty years rolled by, in August 2002, I had some spare money in my pocket and at a vintage car lot, in down town Chico, was a beauty. A real 1930 Model A Ford coupe. Before any deal could be made, I had to make sure of two of the most important items; a rumble seat and a horn that went, ah_ooga. In only moments, I had a name selected for it, Henry Ford and pictures danced in my mind of showing off my dream car, in vintage car shows such as the Concours D' Elegance, held once a year on the Chico State University campus. Then maybe a parade or two with grandkids stuffed inside and in the rumble seat.

This satisfied a dream I've had since childhood, a more sophisticated toy! A toy that beats the Dow! I was recently offered six thousand dollars above what I paid for it.
No sale!

Sometimes the heart is filled with an inner sadness. These are the times for one to grow through the pain and become more and better.

Reflection

Roger E. Honzik

I touched his face and brushed a tear
Within those eyes his sadness clear.
It caused my heart to nearly break.
He touched me then. Oh! My mistake.

It seemed that I should walk on by
To glance away or check the sky
Just never meet him eye to eye
A second look and I would cry.

I first saw him long ago
His deep blue eyes were hurting so
Reflecting me within his eyes
He only begged by asking why.

He was cold, then why not I?
His skin on bone, what hunger I?
I could run, so why not he?
I laughed and pointed, why at he?

His questions came but would not leave
I wore them as though chains indeed.
Wrapped about me year on year
Ever did they hover near.

Then just today I brushed a tear
His face of sadness standing near
For I was shaving on this morn
The mirror held my face half-shorn.

Our first camping trip while living on Bribie Island in Queensland Australia.

A Trip to Remember

Jim Laird

Our family was never much for tent camping so our first excursions into the Australian countryside were usually picnic trips, if over night, staying at motels that were few and far between off the beaten path. Wanting to be able to travel further and be independent I fixed out Volkswagen Van so we could all sleep inside if need be with an extra canvas room attached to the side. With a portable stove, ice chest and folding table we were ready to explore.

We had just heard of an American type rodeo being held a days drive northwest of our home on Bribie Island. With the van packed and ready to go the night before we were off with an early start. We were headed for "Kingaroy" the peanut capital of Australia. It was a pleasant drive on little used roads through a mixture of farms and forest. At lunchtime we stopped at a wide spot beside the road and gathered enough dry branches to fire up our Hibachi and quickly had a nice bed of coals to cook our "Snags" (a fat meat sausage, Australians number one BBQ item). They were eaten before the flies arrived. We noted several spots of interest to visit on the way home when we could be late, not needing a campsite.

A few miles outside Kingaroy several gliders were flying above us. As we were passing the end of a small airport a glider was coming at us flying not much higher than our van. I ducked as it passed overhead coming in for a landing. The wings were making a loud whistle. Several other gliders could be seen on the ground and two in the air. We stopped and returned to watch the action as there was always one or two in the air and others landing or taking off. Having watched gliders from a distance as a kid this is the first time I realized the wings whistled when they were flying. It was an hour well spent. Out campsite was only a couple miles away near a small river. There was no one present when we arrived. Picking a level grassy spot under some large trees not very far from the water tank to camp.

Everyone pitched in to set up our canvas room. We had just completed this when a very strong wind began to blow, tearing branches from trees and shaking the car and canvas room. Never experiencing any thing like this, I had the rest of the family get in the van and close the doors. I stood in the corner of the room facing the wind direction gripping the top frame of the room trying to keep it from blowing away. It was all I could do to keep from being lifted off the ground.

The sides were down so I could not see outside. The wind began to roar and shake the frame and car even harder when I heard a loud bong. The wind suddenly died as quickly as it had arrived. I looked outside to see what had made the big bong, what I saw made my stomach do a flip-flop. The steel top for the water tank was sticking upright in the ground just a foot from where I had been standing. If it had flown any further, it could easily have cut me in half. Keeping my fright from the others we soon had the campsite organized and the nearby wind debris stacked next to the trash containers. Everyone pitched in and we rolled the lid out of the ground and away from our camp where it sat looking like a large Chinese hat laying on the ground. We were lucky the wind and flying branches had not done any damage.

With time on our hands before dark, the boys and I went exploring and found the remains of an old homestead nearby. All the large buildings were gone. Only a small lean-to shed against a cut bank still stood. Looking inside we found many old hand tools lying about that had been abandoned and in very poor condition. Being a collector, I was tempted to adopt them but left them as part of the heritage belonging to the site.

We saw the storms real devastation on our way home two days later. Its path paralleled the highway for miles. In spots where it had touched down in the forest it looked and smelled like a large mower had chopped up all the leaves and small branches leaving the trees standing naked. Instead of smelling like new mowed hay or grass, it smelled like Eucalyptus Cough Syrup. It was then that I realized how lucky we had been to live through a twister. You could see the path where it lifted from the ground and dropped down again. We had been very lucky it had passed over our heads. It skipped over a farmhouse causing little damage, but taking plants out on either side. One of our planned stops was an old homestead preserved as a national park. It was in one of the few remaining stands of Bunya Pine trees. The natives prized the large pine nuts. Local tribes invited other tribes to join them to a large party (called a Cooboree) the years the trees produced nuts. (About every five years). Few of the Pines were damaged probably due to their dense cone shape. A huge brightly colored Poinciana tree in front of the homestead was badly damaged. We lingered so long sticky-beaking the storms damage (being nosy) we only had time to see the outside of the homestead with its wide veranda on all sides of the building set high on wood stumps about eight feet off the ground. The kitchen and bath were under the house and the toilet out back. There are no halls in old homesteads, only doors leading into each room and out to the veranda.

Yes, the Rodeo was good and there were a lot of mean bulls and bucking horses. Yes, the flies and wasps were bad when we cooked breakfast and dinner. The smell of cooking food seems to attract them from miles away and there were so many you could hardly get the food out of the pan much less into your mouth. Bugs, spiders, snakes and big lizards go with the country.

The wash day ritual still burns clearly in my memory. I was probably about four years old when it became clear to me that Monday was ALWAYS (no exception) "Washday."

Memories of Wash Day

Kay Hinerman

My mother's gentle reminder on Sunday nights was some variation of: "Kay, gather up any of your clothes that need washing, and put the clothes basket on the back porch. Tomorrow morning strip your bed when you get up." All soiled clothes and laundry had to be placed in a bushel fruit basket lined with oilcloth by Sunday night and taken to the screened back porch. Sunday night after the evening meal my mother set a boiler on the kitchen woodstove.

This boiler was actually about 40 inches long by 16 to 20 inches deep. It had a tightly fitted lid with huge handles on each end and in the center of the lid. It was made of copper and held eight, 5-gallon milk pails of water. The water was carried from 10- gallon cans of artesian water that were hauled weekly from neighbors. Why? We had no well, as my folks could never get enough money together to have one drilled.

On Monday morning before my mother went to help with the barn chores she built a fire so the water would be boiling when she returned an hour and a half later. After breakfast I did the dishes, and Mom started the wash. First, the clothes were carefully sorted by color. She rolled out a huge wringer washing machine that had a white porcelain-lined tub. This was carefully filled with boiling water dipped into a bucket from the boiler on the stove. The white clothes were added with Fels Naptha Soap grated from a bar. The washer tub agitator was started and the clothes were agitated for exactly 20 minutes. While this was going on, Mom pulled a low table into place next to the wringer side of the washer. Large, round galvanized tubs were placed on top of the table and filled with more water from the boiler.

This was the rinse water. The first tub had water just as hot as what was in the washer; the second was cooled to warm by adding buckets of cold water. After the agitation period, a water-bleached stick was used to pluck the boiling clothes out of the tub and squeeze them through the fat wringer rolls into the first rinse tub. It took some skill to operate the clutch of the wringer and guide the clothes between the rollers without getting a finger caught. As I got older, during summer vacations, it was my job to slosh the clothes through the first rinse and finally, with much caution and a review of how to handle the wringer, roll the clothes through the rollers to the final warm rinse.

From the final rinse the clothes were then wrung into the clothesbasket and taken to the clothesline where they were carefully pinned to dry. Hanging clothes was my job. Clothes were carefully strung together in such a way that one clothespin served to pin two garments. I learned early on if I did it my way, it had to be done over to suit my mother.

Clothes were washed from the whites down to the colored clothing in the next to the last load and finally the Levis, overalls, and work clothing last. Somehow during all this process, my mother washed the delicate clothing that would be ruined in the hot water in the washer. She used cool water, Ivory Flakes, and gently scrubbed the garments on a washboard.

The boiler had to be dried and put away as well as the rinse tubs and the washing machine. All had to be back to normal before noon. This was my mom's rule. I don't know why, and I don't recall ever questioning it.

In the good weather clothes were dry by mid afternoon. They were removed from the clothesline sorted for ironing, folded and put away.

In rainy inclement, weather, clothes were hung on lines in the basement, and the laundry process went on for several days.

Some of rituals from my childhood "washday" carried over into my adult life.

(l) I usually wash only once a week. (2) Hand washing is done without a washboard; (3) A clothes rack on the back deck serves as a clothesline for garments I do not want to put through the dryer.

Most important, doing laundry today is such a "piece of cake" compared to the labor-intensive "Wash Days" of my childhood!

I was raised by immigrant grandparents with the values of Swedish people. I had to do all I could to help.

My Lost Garden

Delores Swenson Squyres

The farm had been sold when I was 14, and my grandmother, my brother and I had moved into town. It was the fall of 1929. My grandmother was happy to leave the farm and all the hard work that living there required

There were no houses near us on our side of the street. I named our house The Cracker box, because it was the same shape, and it was divided into foursquare rooms, just like the crackers in the cracker box. Each room was 12' x 12'. There was no indoor plumbing, even though it was in the city. I carried water for us from a well at the home diagonally across the street. We had an outhouse, with a pot in the house that was used for emergencies.

The house had been the only one my grandmother felt we could afford to rent when we moved to town. My great Uncle William, Administrator of my grandfather's estate, allotted her a small income monthly from the sale of the farm, and she received a small amount of money for my brother and me as wards of the state of Minnesota.

For this reason, my garden was important-it would give us fresh vegetables to eat, which were very expensive at the stores. I had carried the water in buckets from across the street to water it. It had been lots of work, but I was glad to do it! We were going to have plenty of good food!

The early summer morning was so beautiful. I loved being outdoors enjoying it. There was a slight breeze. I had heard that there was a horse show in town, but I had no money for such things, so didn't even think about going. I was happy to be doing my weeding. However, at the same time, I had to keep an eye on my two-year-old cousin Ione, who was living with us at the time. Her mother had died when she was only five days old, and sometimes her father would get angry with the woman who took care of her. Then he would bring her to our grandmother, who always welcomed her.

She kept running out into the street. There wasn't much traffic, but there was some. Bringing her back into the yard kept me from getting the weeding done, and I was getting quite frustrated. Finally someone suggested that I find a small rope, tie one end to the little tree in the front yard, and the other end around her waist. So I did. Then I went back to work. She enjoyed the rope, testing its length and examining it.

Suddenly, a man came racing by. "The wild horses are loose," he screamed as he passed, "and they are headed this way!"

I grabbed a knife I saw-don't know where it came from, and quickly cut the rope, grabbed Ione in my arms, rushed in the front door, and turned around. In seconds, the horses were stampeding through the neighbor's yard, passed their well, and came straight toward our house. There were probably around thirty of them! They speeded across my garden, trampling and destroying everything growing there, and went on into the field behind us and disappeared over the hill.

Ione and I were safe, but the garden was totally destroyed. The delicious food we had anticipated eating was gone, totally eliminated in those few seconds! All my efforts and hard work had been for nothing. Our lives had been spared...Ione's...and mine...but now there would be no fresh vegetables for us.

A lot of us think to play a prank on someone is fun, in someway it is if there is no serious consequence. This story taught me to pause every time I plan some mischief at the expense of others.

Aida

Norma Obitz

No, this is not about the play, it is about Aida, a salesclerk at our store in the Philippines. I do not know how old she was, but she was a lot older than the rest of the clerks. She had these weird sharp eyes that gave you a chill when she looked at you. Her eyebrows were bushy, her nose was long, pointed and bent on the tip. She had a heart shaped face, but very oily. Her lips were full, like Sophia Loren's. She was tall, and had long, gorgeous hair almost to her ankles. She was very proud of it, and combed it almost every hour. She was very bright, and never needed a calculator. I do not know whether it was because of her age, but she did not get along with the rest of the clerks. My brother liked her because she was dependable and efficient.

All of our salesclerks came from my mother's hometown, so I was asked to be nice to them, and I was, most of the time. But I was young, and I could not help being mean and mischievous once in a while. One of my mischiefs almost destroyed my relationship with my mother.

Across from our store was the only bakery in our neighborhood so there were lots of guys employed there. Part of our store was a coffee shop so all of them ate there. They flirted with our salesclerks and some ended in marriages.

I was sixteen when I received my first love letter. I had been dreaming and waiting all my life for my first love letter and to my disappointment it came from one of the guys from the bakery, a baker. I was furious because I knew he was only after my money (like I really have money) and he thought I'd fall for him because he was good looking. I showed the letter to my friend, Baby, and like me, she was mad, too. How dare he, a nobody. This is why we were best friends; we thought, acted, and felt alike.

We acted like we were above every one else in the neighborhood, as if we had been born with silver spoons in our mouths. That was one of the many reasons why our playmates never liked us; even our mothers could not understand why we acted this way.

I did not respond to the letter, but he kept on writing. When I was at the store, he would come over pretending to buy something, flirting with the clerks, hoping I would care. His behavior made me so mad, so Baby and I thought of ways to teach him a lesson. We came up with this brilliant idea; well, we thought it was brilliant, because we did not think of the consequences. We decided we would write love letters to Aida and sign his name. Baby and I dictated the letter:

> *Dear Aida,*
>
> *I know you will be surprised upon receiving this letter and ask yourself why me of all the girls at the store that are younger and a whole lot prettier, but to me beauty is in the eyes of the beholder, and yours is an inner beauty. For months now, I have been watching you, and every day I can see what a marvelous person you are; every day, I learn to care for you more. Please forgive me if this letter is too forward, but I just want to let you know how I feel.*
>
> *Rolly*

You may wonder why I can quote this letter after all these years; at the end of this story you will understand why I will never forget these letters.

Luckily for us, there were two Rollies that worked for the bakery. We did not put a return address or last name, so Aida could not know who had written the letter. Every time I was at the store, I would try to be beside her so that when he looked at me, which he always did, he would be looking in our direction. I would then kind of hint to her that it had to be him because he was always looking at her.

We wrote four more letters, and it started to have an affect on Aida. One day, to everyone's surprise, she cut her gorgeous hair, had it permed, and she wore makeup. She was so happy; she kept on staring at the bakery, waiting for him to notice her. We did not like where this prank was going and were now regretting what we had done. Any sane person would stop at this time, but no, not us. We decided to write one last letter and decided to use the cutting of her hair as our way out. And so we wrote:

Dear Aida,
 The day you cut your hair, I thought my whole world collapsed. The reason why I care for you is that you were unaffected by the fakeness of the world. Your beauty is natural; your gorgeous long hair is what I adored most. I'd never seen anyone with hair like that. Now it is gone and your face is covered with makeup so I do not know you anymore. I guess you did not care for me like I thought you did. I understand, and from now on, I will not bother you anymore.
 Rolly

We were very impressed with the letter; even patted ourselves on the back, thinking this would end what we started.

She received the letter on a Saturday so I was at the store. Tears rolled down her cheeks while reading it, quietly at first, but then it became a non-stop sob.

My mom asked what was wrong, so she handed her the letter. My mom was so furious and decided to go to the bakery.

"Where are you going?" I asked.

" To confront him."

"Who? You don't even know who it is; there are two Rollies in there."

Thank God that stopped her. I now started to panic because Aida was still crying uncontrollably, her whole body was shaking, and worst of all, it was almost lunchtime and they would be coming to eat. I thanked God that Mom decided to take Aida home. I thought everything would be fine. My mom and Aida were home, and my brother was not at the store. Lunchtime came, and as expected, the two Rollies were at the coffee shop. They were eating when my sister in law, the letter in her hand, and not knowing who wrote the letter, decided to confront the two Rollies.

"I don't know which one of you wrote this letter, but if it is only her hair that you want, I will retrieve it from the parlor and tie it around your balls!"

Everyone at the store was mad at them because of Aida but me. I burst into laughter because of the look on the two Rollies' faces. My sister in law was so mad that she had not even noticed me. I thanked God again that the two Rollies just left. I pretended to not know what my sister in law was talking about. .

I thought the worst was over, but Aida really took it hard; she barely ate, and stared at the bakery and cried. My conscience began to bother me, so I decide to tell her the truth. I thought it would ease her pain and everything would be back to normal, but as usual, I was wrong.

"Why are you telling me this, how could you be so cruel? At least before, I felt he cared for me, even for a short time. Now, I know it was just a joke. My life is nothing but a joke," she said, crying as she stormed to the bathroom. She was there for quite a while, so I got worried and told my brother. When he opened the door, he saw Aida holding a bottle of aspirin. We did not know how many she took, but to play it safe we took her to the hospital where she had her stomach pumped, then was released.

Again, I thanked God that we only had aspirin in the cabinet at the time. My prank now turned in to a nightmare. Now everyone knew what I had done. My brother, shaking his head, told Mom and Dad, "She is your child, deal with her." My father in anger for the first time, belted me twice; he hit me so hard, I curled up in pain. But the pain was nothing compared to my Mom's reaction. After assuring them I did not need hospitalization, she asked me if I realized what I had done and what could have happened. My smart answer was, "But nothing happened; her pain could not be worse that what I'm feeling right now." Mom looked at me sadly and said, "You are not even sorry; I don't know what I did to have a child like you."

The next day Aida quit and went back to the province. My brother disliked me more when she left because he lost his right hand at the store. It was not really all bad. When Aida went back to the province, she found the love of her life after a year. My brother even paid for their wedding. He is really not as bad as I portrayed him to be. Aida is not mad at me anymore; she is even thankful and named their first baby after me. She said if it had not been for me, she would still be at the store, she would not have met her husband, and probably be an old maid. To tell you the truth, because of the happy ending, everyone with the exception of my parents, thought what I did was very funny. They could not stop laughing when we told them what my sister in law said to the two Rollies.

I write for the fun of writing and hopefully, someone will enjoy what I have written.

Living Alone Among People

Ellen Eagar

I never realized while growing up that I was growing up alone, even though I seemed to have friends. Of course while I was young I was always close to my mother so that she would know that I was safe.

I was raised in a family of five in the state of Florida. My brother and sister were five and seven years older than myself so we had no interests in common. My father was a civil engineer with the road department, building roads in different locations, and of course the family also moved along. In fact, in one instance, we had to live in a tent until we could find a place to live. We lived as far west as Pensacola, as far south as Miami, and as far north as Jacksonville.

We never managed to stay in one town more than a year, so every year it was necessary for me to make new "friends". Small towns had no playgrounds as they do today, so if we moved in the summer, it was hard on us children, particularly if there were no children in the neighborhood. I never went to one school more than a year at a time until I reached high school. Sometimes I returned to a town where I had lived, and then I would have some friends I had known before.

One time when I was in high school, we returned to a town where we had lived so often, that we called it home. There I had good friends, I thought.

It was at this time that the young people began drinking and smoking and I wanted no part of that. My so-called "friends" let me know that I was no longer welcome in the group. Luckily, even though it was a small town, I was able to meet new friends. But for the first time, it made me feel like an outsider.

As I became more mature, I would hear people reminisce about things they had done together as children and teens. This was a pleasure I never had.

When I married, I continued to live outside looking in, as I had married a navy man. My husband, Joe, was on patrol planes so we were almost always together somewhere on dry land, but we moved to a new location almost every two years.

It was an interesting life and I saw lots of places within the United States. The only time I was overseas was when we were first married. Joe was stationed in Trinidad, B.W.I., and I flew down there to marry him. We were stationed there for three years. We met very few people we called friends. In fact, there are only two couples that we still keep in touch with.

After twenty-two years in the navy, Joe retired and we returned to his hometown of Denver, Colorado, where he found work with the Martin-Marietta Company. I also found work and for ten years we had a home, which was good for our growing family. However, after ten years, the contract ran out and the company sent us to California to work on the Titan II missile at Vandenberg Air Force Base.

Two years later, when that contract ran out, it was time once again to make a move. By now our three children were in high school, and I wanted this to mean something to them.

Joe and I were on our way to Washington State, but we stopped in Chico for a cup of coffee. Joe picked up a paper, found a couple of items of interest, so we spent the night. The next day he found work in Paradise, so we returned to Santa Maria to collect our children and belongings and we moved to Paradise. We found a place to live and this is where we have remained. It was good for the children and good for us. They made friends and we did too. They have become our good friends, which has been proven many times. And this is what we needed.

I realize now how much I missed while I was growing up. Our life in the Navy and our motorcycling has brought us many acquaintances all over the United States and Canada, but our friends are here in Paradise.

My maternal grandparents and great grandparents were from Sweden, where the Lutheran Church was of great importance in their lives. It was essential that we attend church every Sunday if at all possible. I went to live with my grandparents when I was two years old, so attended many years of services at this church.

The Church of My Childhood

Delores Swenson Squyres

    This church had a strong influence on my life-then-- and as I grew up, and it continued in my adult life. There are many people who have no concept as to the deep influence it can have on a child's life- even one who seems to be paying no attention whatsoever.

    This church is located a few miles south of the town of Kandiyohi, in Kandiyohi County, in the state of Minnesota. We lived five miles from the church, which made it a really difficult task to get there for Sunday services, or at other times. Only a small part of the roads driven were graveled. Most were dirt roads, which were very muddy when it rained or the snow melted. But getting there was an absolute necessity to my grandparents. That was part of their heritage.

    My grandparents had two carriages that I particularly remember, but those were not suitable when there were too many of us, and were seldom used. In the winter, the wagon was turned into a sled, with runners replacing the wheels.

    The bottom of the wagon or sled was covered with hay, making it soft to sit or lie on. We covered up with heavy blankets and real bear rugs that had been made from bears that had been killed on the farm. Of course, we all wore caps or hats, mittens or gloves, and warm coats. We were dressed for cold winter weather.

    Pete and Prince were the team of horses that most often took us to church. When it snowed, my grandfather would put the snowbells on them. How us kids loved to hear them ring! I wonder how long it took us to go that five miles in the sled? I know I often fell asleep and slept most of the way, snuggled up under that warm, cozy rug, enjoying the fragrance and softness of the hay under me. Since Sunday school started at 10 A.M. and church Services at 11 A.M., we must have left home very early in the morning!

When we arrived at the church, we all got out of the sled, brushed the hay off our clothes, and went into the church. My grandfather would take the team to the barns-each family owned their own section of the barn, my mother had purchased one for my grandfather's use-unhitched them, and put them in the barn. Did he feed the horses? I think so, but I never saw him do it. Then he came into the church.

The church had a full basement with a large kitchen that had several large cook stoves. The rest of the basement was an entrance area, and then one big room, where various meetings and meals were enjoyed. An annex had been built behind and adjoining the church. One could go from it into the main church through the minister's study. Sunday school classes were held in either the basement or the annex. After Sunday school, we all went into the church.

There were quite a few steps to climb as one entered the church. It had been built quite high, which allowed the basement to have windows, allowing light and sun to enter. As one entered the church, there was a hall with hooks for hanging coats. Overshoes were placed on the floor below the coats.

I always felt that the church was very beautiful. I spent many hours studying the three stained glass windows on each side of the church and the picture of Jesus at the front. As one entered the church through the swinging doors, the pulpit was to the left and slightly ahead of the platform that divided the congregation from the alter and the semi-circular communion rail in front of it. A center aisle divided the pews. A piano was on the platform on the right, in the front. In the front, at platform level, were two very small rooms, one on each side, with doors into the church and connecting with the annex. That's where the minister put on his robes before entering to conduct the services. At the back, stairs were provided on either side of the area, that lead up to the balcony seating and the pipe organ.

All the children came into the church with the parents after Sunday school. We all had received Sunday School papers to read, and parents urged children to do so when they became restless during the sermon, which took place between the ritual parts of the service. The sermon was often very long. At this little country church, Sunday services were sometimes conducted in Swedish.

I still recall vividly a sermon preached one Sunday when I was around seven years old, on the narrow and the wide roads, about how easy and attractive the wide road was, and how narrow and sometimes very difficult the narrow one was. The minister would get loud and emphatic, and he'd swing his arms and hammer them with great gusto. But I didn't look at him very much. I was really picturing that wide road, where everything was easy and fun, and then the narrow road, where one had to obey many rules and follow the teachings of Jesus. It sounded like that wide road would be so much fun! Yet I was drawn to the narrow road, as I pictured it, with Jesus traveling it with me. I can still picture it in my mind even today-over 80 years later. It deeply influenced my life when things got real difficult and I was tempted to take the easier path knowing it would be wrong. I thank God for that sermon-even all these many years later!

II.
Bring On The Clowns
Voices of Laughter

The Black Cat Cafe

Ariel Edmundson

An off-beat place on Montgomery Street,
Where the gay ones meet.
Their voices rise in falsetto speech,
Trying to bridge the incredible breach,
Sawdust on the floor, abstract paintings
on the wall,
A Bohemian setting awaits the fairies ball.

This story of mine shows our kids how the world changes. What we went through when we were kids to read something we were not allowed to. Today all they have to do is click a mouse and they can read, see and know everything, but is it to their advantage? It also teaches us that there are times adults know best.

The Book

Norma Obitz

It brings a smile to my face when I think of the stupidest thing that Baby, Mia and I did during our second year in high school.

It was at that time that "Fanny Hill" was the "must" book to read in the school. Almost everyone had read it and those who hadn't, were dying to read it. No one called it Fanny Hill; it was known as "The Book".

One morning at the cafeteria, Cynthia, one of the most popular senior girls at school, and her group of friends were reading it. They pretended to be reading a magazine but we all knew they were reading 'The Book". They were giggling, ooh-ing, saying, "'Read this part, read this part!" and showing it to one another then uttering "Oh my God, oh my God, oh no!" Mia and I were at the table across from them, staring, wondering what was in the book that made them act like idiots. Mia could not stand it, so she went to their table and asked if we could see what they were reading. Cynthia just looked at her and said, "This book is for women only, not for children". Mia and I were short, so most students thought we were still in our first year. Furious, Mia yelled, "Do you think you are the only one who can afford to buy the book?" Cynthia replied "Kids never listen to grownups; for the last time, kids are not allowed to read this so you can't buy it." Mia returned to our table still furious saying, "It is just a lot of hogwash that we can't buy the book."

The book had been on Mia's mind all day so we planned to cut afternoon classes the next day and go downtown. I really did not want to go downtown because chances of being caught by my father were great. He went to movies practically every day and the theaters were in the downtown area, but having the book seemed to be important to Mia.

The next day we went downtown, entered a bookstore and searched for the book on the shelves but could not find it. Mia told me to go ask the sales clerk. "Why me? You are the one who wants to buy the book," I said. "Because you are older". She replied. "Only two months; besides, you are taller so you look older than I," I answered back. Other customers started staring at us so Mia went to the clerk and said, "I want to buy "Fanny Hill". Where can I find it?"

The clerk looked at her and said, "Your nose is still dripping and you want to read Fanny Hill?"

I don't know why, but back then every time kids wanted to do something they were not supposed to do, or want things they are not supposed to have, that would be the grown-ups' reason. "Because your nose is still dripping." The clerk's attitude towards us made me mad, so trying to act like an adult, I said, "Excuse me sir, I am seventeen and she is eighteen, so do not treat us like children."

"Yeah, right," he said mockingly. "I am sorry I did not realize you are dwarves, still you have to be twenty one to buy it. I tell you what, judging by your uniform you are at least fourteen miles away from your school, so either you cut class or did not go at all. Maybe I should call your parents and inform them that their dwarves want to buy Fanny Hill." He stopped to stare at us and then continued. "Nah, on second thought I should just call the cops. You know the penalty for dwarves who buy this book is Life." That was all he had to say; we ran out the store as fast as we could. It was really not the cops but the calling of my parents that scared me the most.

I thought that would be the end of it, but Mia's fascination about the book was unrelenting. Every day she would think of ways to get hold of it, so finally I told her I could ask Baby to buy it for us. Baby, though three months younger than we were, was almost two feet taller than I. Kids in the neighborhood called us Mutt and Jeff. We talked to Baby about it and she agreed because she herself was curious about the book; it seemed like everybody at school had read it except us.

We made several plans on how to get the book. Plan A, Baby would try to buy it from the bookstore, that is if she could pass for twenty-one, which was nearly impossible because all of us were just fourteen at the time. Plan B would be to get it from a newsstand where they sold Playboy and other smuts, so we figured they would have it and they were kind of lax on obeying laws. We didn't want a passerby to see us buying it. We decided to do it on the weekend because if we skipped class and had to roam around downtown in search of a newsstand that sells the book, for sure I would bump into my father, and that would be the end of my life. Not only would I be grounded forever, it would definitely end my school life. So one Saturday, pretending to go to movies, we began our hunt for "The Book".

We went to another bookstore this time, and since it was Saturday it was very crowded. Mia and I got a magazine and Baby, pretending not to be with us, approached the clerk and asked in a very soft and polite voice, " Do you carry "Fanny Hill?" The clerk looked at her then yelled, "Hey June, this kid wants to know if we carry "Fanny Hill." We were stunned by the clerk's action. Everyone in the store started cracking up and looked at Baby. She was red as a tomato and almost in tears. Mia and I just looked at her helplessly trying to think of what to do, when suddenly we realized she was gone.

We ran out of the store after her but could not find her. I was crying and started blaming Mia, telling her I lost the only real friend I had. She was also crying and said, "Yeah, then what am I to you?" We then realized we were making a scene so we stopped and continued to look for Baby.

We found her three blocks from the store standing on the corner waiting for us. I started apologizing but she had already calmed down and said, "We have to get that book even if it kills us." So we started cruising the streets, looking for a newsstand that sold the book.

I can't remember how many blocks we walked, but finally we found a place that carried it. "The Book" occupied almost half of the stand; you could not miss it. Luckily for us, the owner was an older woman, so we felt a little better. Baby boldly approached the stand, took "The Book" and paid for it. That was all there was to it, after all the humiliation, just like that, we now had "The Book." We immediately inserted the book into the magazine. Now our problem was where to read it. Not in our homes, because none of us had our own bedroom, so we decided to go to the park. We found the perfect place away from the crowd and we started reading. I can't remember how far we read but we finally stopped because it was starting to gross us out. We looked at each other and said, "Ugh, is this what married people do?" We closed the book and decided to go home.

None of us wanted to take the book home so we dumped it in the trash. We were laughing all the way home and talking about what a day we had. We now understood why the book was not for kids, and for the first time we agreed that grown-ups were right this time, and that we would understand and maybe enjoy the book more when we turned twenty-one.

We never forgot that day. Every time the three of us get together, we just burst into laughter, remembering that day. When Mia got married, Baby and I tried to find a copy of "Fanny Hill", but we couldn't find it; so we settled for "Lady Chatterley's Lover." We put a cover on the book and wrote, "Fanny Hill" on it. That was our gag gift to her so she wouldn't forget that it was she who caused us the embarrassment that none of us will ever forget.

Written for my grandchildren. My mother always told me that mothers have eyes in the back of their heads!

Mother's Wisdom

Florence Johanson

My mother always told me
When I was very small,
"The last thing you want to be when you grow up
Is a "Know It All!"
"No one will like you -
You won't have a single friend,
You'll never get married.
You must learn to blend!"

Now, I wasn't sure, when all was said and done,
That I knew what a " know it all" was
But I knew, I'd better never become one!

As I grew older and went to school,
I thought that my teacher
Must not know my mother's rule.

She seemed to be trying her best
To make me learn everything
She never gave it a rest!
I tried to resist
So that I wouldn't become too smart,
But that just made my mother mad!
She took my teacher's part!

So I learned to hide some things
That I thought were clever,
Like sneaking candy, reading under the covers
Running away to the alley, and others!

Then one day, I had a rude awakening
When I finally confessed to my mother
These things I thought long hidden.
She just looked at me with a gentle smile
And said, "Dear, I knew it all the while."

That's when I felt it--
A horror I can clearly now recall--
My OWN mother was a "know it all"!

At an early age my grandmother taught me very practical solutions to some of life's problems. This story is an example of one of the great lessons I learned from her.

Rooster Savvy
Kay Hinerman

The year I was nine I learned a great deal about fear. My parents had sold the sheep ranch as my dad's health was failing. We moved into a rental house with only five acres as a "temporary stop" until a suitable, smaller ranch could be found and purchased.

That fall I was saddled with many problems. I wanted so much to have a piano and take lessons. There was no money for that luxury, but mom suggested I take violin lessons through the school on a violin that had been in her family long before my time.

I was not thrilled about learning to play the violin, but it was a musical instrument, and perhaps I would learn to read music. The music teacher at the school was a student of the violin, and she was delighted with the opportunity to teach her instrument of choice. I carried the violin case back and forth to school each day as children who were working on a special instrument had a 40-minute time to practice.

My parents, upon moving, had bought a large flock of New Hampshire Red hens and three roosters. Their plan was to sell eggs to a local hatchery. The three roosters sported plumage fit for a milliner's shop. The long curving tail feathers were a beautiful dark auburn, which blended out to a blue-black the last few inches. The feathers on the body were thick with a molten look of hot coals. In addition to their strong sinewy legs and sharp talon-like toes, they had two long sharp spurs on each leg that were vicious weapons when they were provoked to fight with each other. They were almost as tall as I was, and I hated them at first sight. I believe they spent their days preening and strutting and waiting for me to come home from school. I was loaded down with books, a paper bag of sheet music, and of course the violin case.

The first day after the roosters came to live my passage from the front gate to the back door became one of terror. I had to turn my back to the house as I latched the front gate, then walk around the side of the garden, into the back yard where the roosters resided. My appearance in the yard was their signal to come running to investigate! One ran at high speed with his head and neck parallel to the ground and his wings spread. He was a fearful sight. My heart was in my throat as I screamed at him. When he got close I bopped him with the paper bag of music. It ripped, dropped, and music went flying all over the yard. This caught the attention of a second rooster and he came running to investigate. I swung at him with the violin case, missed, and dropped the case. He then flew at my legs with his spurs flared ready to fight.

I raced him to the back door; a race I won, but I was hysterical. The back yard looked like a war zone with schoolbooks, sheet music, and a violin case now burst open strewn around.

My mother scolded me for dropping my school things and told me to "get out there and get them picked up!"

How was I going to go back into that area where the enemy lived? I convinced my dad if he would pick up my things for me this once I would never let it happen again. Oh, how I hated those roosters! What could I do? I cried and sobbed, but that didn't help.

The next day I went to my grandmother's after school. She listened intently to my problem. She said I had to show the roosters that I was the boss. She said she thought she could help me out. Gram had an old squirt gun that she filled with soapsuds. She told me to shoot them in the eyes; if I missed it would get in their face and on their beaks and they would leave me alone. Further, she said to hide the gun by the front gate and shake the solution up good when I picked it up each day so it would be soapy.

"Your mom and dad don't have to know about this." "And something else," she said, "keep it loaded with soap suds." Then she said something I'll always remember: "Walk like you are the boss. Animals can smell fear. You must not act like you are a 'fraidy cat'."

It worked. I had no more trouble with the roosters. Gram saved the day and taught me a valuable lesson.

Collector's Item

Dawn McFarland

The first three years of her life she collected:
dubious complaints of "What a pretty little boy;"
measles, noisiness, weight, vitality and
the contents of other people's pockets.

From three to five she collected:
a fondness for nursery school, long curls, dimples, a tricycle,
curiosity, other people's hearts and the chicken pox!

At five she started collecting little brothers;
dresses in place of jeans, schoolmates and French braids.

From eight to eleven she collected
a good many A's in spelling, many hours of baby sitting
and her mothers gratitude for being a girl.

Came adolescence she collected the
startling world of boys - other than brothers - telephone calls
and a surprisingly strict pair of squares called parents.
Plus a strong suspicion that all was not well with the universe.

A few hours ago she collected"
Her first long dress, her first permanent,
And a tear from her mother's eye as she kissed
a lovely young woman
who bore no resemblance to the little girl
once mistaken for a boy.

Farm life for children in 1916 was a constant adventure that combined ingenuity and mischief with the profound learning that hard work could be enjoyed but not taken too lightly.

Not In My Watermelon Patch

Lois C. Adams

In 1916, the year I was seven, we had a wonderful watermelon patch. It was near the pond Dad had built beside the small river which ran through the lower edge of the farm. It was separated from the river by a barbed wire fence, broken only by an access gate. Dad had arranged for the sale of the melons, and they were just beginning to ripen. It was fun to run from melon to melon, tapping them to listen for that ripe sound.

But mysteriously, at about that time, the melons began to disappear and Dad found some partly eaten melons in the patch. We found large footprints, and Dad reasoned that they belonged to some male high school students.

One day Mom and Dad had me "help" them prepare the big flat hay rick for camping out under the stars that night. We had fun carrying to the rick big, dusty loads of hay, which they arranged evenly on the wagon bed as a mattress. Then they spread a large tarp, and on that, sheets, blankets and a couple of bottles of drinking water for children who might get thirsty during the night.

With three giggling children aboard, Dad drove the team of horses down the farm road toward the river, and parked the rick near the watermelon patch. He removed two large rolls of strong twine which he always had on hand for many uses. As Mother unhitched the horses and drove them back to the barn, we children watched Dad patiently string the twine back and forth, among the watermelons. When he had used up most of his twine, he ended with four ends at the wagon. By tying a couple of bells to the wagon end of each piece of twine, then tying the ends to the wagon, he could tell the location of the thieves.

To make the adventure more exciting, Mom had prepared a picnic supper, which we ate as we sat on the biggest watermelons we could find, being very careful not to pull on a string. Dad had already done that, to show us how it would sound if the culprits invaded the melon patch.

After we arranged ourselves comfortably on the wagon bed, our clothes piled in a little row across the seat, we snuggled under the sheets. Counting the stars, trying to remember Mom's names for them, and listening to her stories, we finally fell asleep.

Some time after midnight, Caryl, who was only three, awakened with, "Mama, I have to go potty." By the time she was back in her hay bed, we were all awake, whispering so we wouldn't alert the thieves, should they appear.

We were getting very sleepy, and I think Gordon and Caryl were asleep, when one pair of bells began to ring. In short order, the other three bells were jingling, very irregularly. Dad stood up in his long nightgown, reached up to the wagon seat and brought down the shotgun. "Oh, don't kill them, Daddy," I whispered. He quickly assured us he was only going to scare them by shooting into the sky. And he did, with his shotgun explosions ringing out threateningly, blending with intermittent ringing of the bells, as people scrambled for what they hoped would be an exit. Just before all became quiet in the melon patch, we heard some bursts of profanity, and some grunts and moans. Then some giggles from youthful male voices.

The next day was Monday. As we drove our Ford touring car past the melon patch, we saw the wagon still standing there with our bedding piled up, and the hay in a neat stack in the center, to be taken back to the barn for the animals to eat. We began reliving the night's adventure, and it kept us entertained the whole three miles to the Minersville schoolhouse, where I was a second grader and Dad was the Superintendent. His office was in the high school part of the building, and the first order of the day was an assembly.

Marching in late, as the assembly was just beginning to sing and have a short meeting, came seven or eight older boys, most with revealing scratches on their arms and faces, all looking very embarrassed. Dad took no notice of them.

Shortly after assembly ended, when Dad arrived at his office, some very sheepish and apologetic boys waited at his door.
Dad explained the economics of his watermelon crop, and suggested that he would need some watermelon pickers soon, when the crop was really ripe. Every one of those boys forsook his life of crime and for the next two years happily helped us at harvest time.

I am fascinated by, and envious of, those who are super-organized. What would we do without them?

The Dutiful

Barbara Lang

There are people among us - I'd like to be one,
You know, those good folk who get things done.
Their works are impeccable, leaving nothing to chance,
They know what they're doing well in advance.
Their tax forms are filed by mid-March, never late
(So unlike us poor mortals, who procrastinate.)
Each sensible action is done within reason,
They purchase new clothes only off-season.
Volunteering to serve on Committees,
They work hard to improve their cities.
Calendars full, scheduled down to each minute,
Reminders unneeded, these creatures of habit.
Their compulsive behavior I find most incredible,
Whose cabinets hold spices arranged alphabetical.
They who in spring, actually do the spring cleaning
By mid summer they're done Christmas shopping.
Those whose menus are planned, not accidental,
Food only purchased from lists, how mechanical!
In duties performed they seem inexhaustible
Oh, if only I could be so infallible.
But, alas, Society holds those blameless
Who are anti-spontaneous.

The monthly evening out to dinner with my husband Lou's, drywall construction crew and their wives.

Who Goes First

Bee Mandell

This evening was different. It was at a new elegant Polynesian restaurant. A new couple, Dale and Karen, joined us. They said they were newlyweds. The men on the crew doubted it.
We were seated at a long table facing another couple in our party of eight. Service was family style for each set of couples. Our partners were Dale and Karen. I have set the scene. Now the fun began. A large six-tier server loaded with exotic appetizers was placed in the middle of the table before each set of couples.
Lou and I, to be polite suggested, "You go first."
Karen cooed, "You go first dear."
"Oh, no," Dale said, "You go first sweetheart."
"I couldn't. You go first, lover."
After a few rounds of that, Lou and I quickly became disenchanted with the "you go first" and dug in. When we figured we had gobbled our share, we suggested it was their turn. They remained stuck on "you go first."
We started nibbling on the balance of the appetizers. They didn't seem to notice, even when the waiter removed the empty server.
Next came a large tureen of soup and individual bowls.. To the tune of hugs and kisses and "you go first," we polished that off. The rest of our party were enchanted and royally entertained as Lou and I devoured the salad and main courses. The couple seemed oblivious.
The waiters struggled to conceal their laughter.
Lou and I were rather full, but we had good appetites in those days. We even managed to enjoy the four helpings of dessert.
During the after dinner period of relaxed conversation, Dale and Karen graduated to hug, kisses., and cuddling.
Monday morning at work the men asked Dale how they enjoyed the dinner.
Dale said, "The restaurant was nice, but we were so hungry when we left we had to stop at a fast food place for something to eat. I wonder who went first?" .

This story is about living in my neighborhood during prohibition.

Bathtub Beer
Jim Laird

The great American experiment of Prohibition did not work. An old expression "Where there is a will there is a way" fit the times very well. Despite all the government efforts expressed later on the TV show "Elliot Ness" as played by Robert Stack, our county would not dry up. Stills in the hills of the south and east were busy making illegal alcohol. Drivers delivering the alcohol challenged the government to catch them using cars they created to go faster than those of the government. These cars turned to racing when prohibition ended to become the NASCAR races seen on TV most Sundays.

As a 7and8 year old living on Elsie St. in Los Angeles during this period, this is what I remember. Hard liquor was in evidence everywhere. Almost every weekday afternoon, Ray, a neighbor returning home from work, would weave his way along the sidewalk. It was obvious he was making an effort to walk normally. He would stop and check his pocket making sure his bottle was secure. His unsteady hand would fumble it. The bottle sometimes slipped from his fingers and crashed to the sidewalk, leaving a puddle of liquid and broken glass. Staring down at the mess on the sidewalk with a blank look for a moment, he'd then continue down the sidewalk, head held high with an innocent "know nothing look".

Nick, another neighbor driving home after work, often stopped at a café a few blocks from home and left feeling no pain. It was just across the street from the store where Ray worked and was known locally to have alcohol available. Nick's wife worried about his drinking when it was late for him to be home. She would call me from her front porch (our playground was the street) and give me a nickel to get him. For me, it was an easy nickel as I got to ride back in his car. I would pause after opening the café door to give him time to see me. He never stalled as I walked into the café and he met me near the door.

We always made it safely home, probably because there was little traffic in those days.

Beer was the choice alcoholic drink for most of the neighborhood. The ingredients to make beer must have been inexpensive and easy to get because so many made it. It was brewed in the family bathtub. Neighbors took turns, as their bathtub was unusable while making beer. This was not a real inconvenience as most families only took baths once a week. It was during the depression and money was scarce and hard to get. Water heaters were only lit on bath days to save money on gas. The bathtub was the right size to make a batch of beer large enough for a neighborhood party. How well the tub was cleaned before the brewing started, I don't know. Maybe the alcohol was supposed to sanitize it! The beer was never bottled but dipped right from the tub when it was ready. It gave off a distinct odor that your nearest neighbor could smell and the news was passed around because everyone seemed to know when it was ready. Families with little kids brought them on party night and they were bedded in the family beds or on the floor. Boys on one end, girls on the other if need be.

 My dad decided to try and do it a little different one time. He was working regular and could afford to buy some large crocks, bottles and a capper. He set his operation up on our back porch. I was given the impression he was making root beer. It did not smell like root beer to me. When he thought the beer was ready, he filled the bottles and I helped him cap them. He set the bottles one at a time under the capper, placing a cap on top. I would use all my weight to push the capper handle down, pressing the cap on tightly. The bottles were stored in the pantry next to our icebox. It used real ice to cool.

 A few days later, I heard some loud noises near the back of the house and thought someone was shooting a gun. When dad came home, I told him about hearing someone shooting nearby. He rushed to the pantry and opened the door to see broken beer bottles lying around in the wet remains of his beer. In his rush to make and bottle his beer before the neighbors knew about it, he had bottled it while it was still green and fermenting, causing the bottles to explode. He did made another batch in his crocks and we had a neighborhood party. No more bottles to explode. We could use the bathtub anytime.

I find that the best way for me to handle approaching senility is to acknowledge it myself, thereby beating others to the punch at pointing out my increasing frailties.

Ah, How Well I Don't Remember

Karen Romig

Have you heard the story about the elderly man who was telling a friend about a memory-improvement class he was taking? "It's great!" he exclaimed. "It's all about word association. All you have to do is think of a word that you can associate with something you want to remember, and it comes to you, just like that!."

"Sounds terrific!" replied his friend. "What's the instructor's name?"

After a brief pause, the first guy asked "What do you call that flower that smells really good but has thorns on it?"

"You mean a rose?"

"Yeah, that's it!" said the first man, turning toward the kitchen. "Hey, Rose, what's the name of that guy who teaches the memory course I'm taking?"

You think that's funny, do you? Well just wait a couple of years til it happens to you; I guarantee you won't be laughing any longer. Somebody or something has been taking the words right out of my mouth for a year or two now, and it's driving me bananas!

The overly mature mind is a fascinating, fearsome, frustrating thing. At least mine is. Fascinating, however, only to a clinical psychologist; for me, it's the other two "F" words.

For instance, I remember a kid-type radio program when I was three that started "I am your luncheon, yum-yummy, yum-yummy, and I'm coming down to visit your tummy".

The tummy-visiting luncheon I had today is beyond recall. I can sing the entire Cream of Wheat song and intro to the "Let's Pretend" radio show that I listened to when I was six or so, but I can't recall a TV program I enjoyed yesterday.

Dates? I remember the birthdays of classmates I didn't even hang around with, but I have trouble with my own kids' birthdays, let alone those of my grandchildren. And don't EVER ask me their ages - I stopped keeping track as soon as my oldest daughter became older than I am. There are days when I have to check my computer to see what day it is before checking my calendar to see what 's on the docket for the day. Sometimes I forget where I left the calendar. I've been known to lose entire weeks that way.

A couple of us were discussing favorite Theater on the Ridge productions just this morning. She mentioned her favorite by name. I've already forgotten what she said, but remembered when she named it that I had liked it too. I haven't the foggiest what it was about. I've also forgotten the name of my personal pet production - and I saw it twice. I couldn't remember it this morning either, but said it was about a quartet. My friend immediately knew and named it, but I don't remember what she said. Maybe it will come to me later, maybe not.

Having a mind like mine is extremely hard work! Paperwork gets lost and has to be redone, sometimes several times. Precious time and energy are often expended in thinking up excuses for forgetting a name, a promise, or a project. Looking for things I've misplaced is nothing short of an adventure! I almost never find what I'm looking for, but I'm very likely to turn up something I lost months or even years ago. This year I'm not going to buy a single Christmas gift before December first. I recently ran across six items on a closet shelf that I forgot I had bought as gifts. The intended recipients got something else this year, and by next year these things will probably no longer be suitable or appropriate.

News from friends is a nightmare! For instance, one friend will tell me about a planned trip to Greece, another will report on a scheduled surgical procedure, yet another will offer specifics on a recent death of a spouse or an impending divorce. Within a day I will have forgotten who's doing or having what. The sadder the news, the faster I forget. My brain's ability to blot out bothersome details is remarkable. I seem to have developed a natural immunity to retainment of stressful news. Whatever I don't remember, it seems, never happened. Therefore I try not to ask any leading questions, such as, "What's your husband up to these days?" There's a good chance said husband ran off with his best friend's wife or was run over by a truck or died of a long-term illness. Worse yet, I was probably informed of it in excruciating detail shortly after it took place.

In order to keep my level of embarrassment at an absolute minimum without seeming unfeeling and unfriendly, I've tried to work up a few non-incriminating questions, such as "Tell me all about this latest excitement in your life" or "Fill me in again about so-and-so - I've forgotten the details." Sometimes this works, often it doesn't, whereupon the egg on my face raises my cholesterol to a perilous level.

There is one good thing about a mind like mine: I'm perfectly safe with secrets and vicious gossip. You can tell me in great detail about an affair you're having with a very married man. I may remember the affair, but not who's having it with whom. Of course, there's always the chance I'll remember a name and not the activity. A business lunch with your boss could become a rendezvous in Reno by the time I find someone to tell it to. It's a calculated risk.

People often comment on the fact that I'm always smiling. This bothers me. I know I smile a lot; so does a complete idiot. I suspect neither of us has a clue as to why we're grinning. We'd like to know, but we can't remember...

This poem points to what was once a hobby, but is now a drive to reach deep within and strive to understand.

My Pleasure

Roger E. Honzik

Graced as if by simple plan
Laid down within the quiet sand
Of time before the birth of man
To walk in toil on this land.

Was it struck that I should write
In gentle rhyme to some delight
All conjured here from deep within
As feelings well and flows begin?

I question not the drug within
Which causes word and mind to spin
As rhythms grip my very soul
Which soon may birth a timid foal.

Only that some rhyme to me,
Oh hapless man, so simple be
That even words I'm pressed to see
Are vexing vagrants shunning me.

Yet mornings long before the birds
These voices wake with stirring words
And cause me to pursue them all
As polished thoughts they may befall.

So write I do as well I must
A lowly man I walk in trust
This course on which I ever be
By fate or God that pleasures me.

Did you ever wonder about the origin of warning signs? Read on!

Splaalaat!

Marion Williams

It was two days before Christmas in 1999, and I was visiting my son and his family in Canyon Country, a hilly area north of Los Angeles. Susie, my daughter-in-law, and I were going to the mall for some last-minute shopping. I was waiting for her to back the car out of the garage before I got into the car. Suddenly, she remembered something she needed to take with her, and she dashed back into the house.

Noticing that the rubbish truck had already made its pick up, I decided to take the trash containers into the back yard. I pushed the large wheeled container, used only for vegetation, down the street and up the driveway into the back yard. With my large purse in one hand, I grabbed the handle of the second container--a huge ninety-six gallon can on wheels--one used for all the household waste. I started to push the trash can down the street, so I could wheel it up the driveway instead of going over the curb. Apparently my hand slipped off the handle. The can flipped over and started rolling down the hill. The cover flew open, and I tripped over the handle. I was flung headlong into the smelly trash can! I was still hanging onto my purse, and only my feet were sticking out of the can. As I struggled to get out of the can, I wondered who might have seen me. I thought of what a big laugh Daniel and Amanda, my grandchildren, would have had if they had seen their grandmother in the trash can. I also thought that it would have been a prize winner on "Funniest Home Videos." Somehow I really hoped none of the neighbors had seen me!

My injuries were several large black and blue marks, a sprained finger, bruised shoulder, and skinned calves. The most serious injury was my wounded pride!

Addendum: A few months later I got a big chuckle when I saw a decal had been placed on the trash can. The sign, printed in both English and Spanish, said: "Caution!" User may trip when rolling cart with lid open. Close lid before rolling cart. Apparently other people have gone "splaalaat!"

My mother on her 99th birthday.

I Cry For My Mother

Florence Johanson

I cry for my mother but no one hears.
I cry for my mother-silent, futile tears.

We light the candles she cannot blow.
Read cards from people she does not know.

I pat her shoulder and kiss her cheek.
Her eyes are vacant-she cannot speak.

She struggles to express a thought, to say a word.
I struggle to make her think that I have heard.

My mother is gone and in her place
Is an empty shell with a wrinkled face.

A shriveled body with life burning low.
I love you, Mother. I hope you know.

Searching for anything chocolate one evening, I found a handful of stale chocolate chips left over from Holidays, and wrote this poem.

The Seduction

Barbara Lang

I love thee, my Chocolate, so very much
You are good to the smell, the taste, and the touch.
My passion for you, O Coco Bean, one could compare
To that of an illicit love affair.
I am stripped of all pride, unabashedly amorous,
Have you NO faults, injurious or noxious?
Smooth, brown temptress, always delectable,
When covered by you, lowly prunes are acceptable.
At once food of angels, and also the devil,
Would that you be more bland, more unpalatable.
If tomorrow the country banned you, O my Chocolate,
Hersey Kisses would be sold on the black market.
Though I vow to be rid of thee
You taunt me and tease me.
Without you I'm useless and melancholic
A candidate in rehab for chocoholics.
Tantalizing, addictive, seductive, I say,
Ought not you be banned by the FDA?

Baking skills were a huge challenge for me; probably the one that gave me the most trouble was the art of making light, fluffy pastry.

The Pie Crust Lesson

Kay Hinerman

I had been married about two years when we were invited to dinner at the home of one of Jim's friends. I had looked forward all week to the dinner, as I had never met Gene, the friend, or his wife, Joyce.

We arrived at the designated time, and I was surprised to see Joyce was making a lemon meringue pie for dessert! I hadn't made many pies at this point in my married life, but I recalled my mother's pies were always made several hours to a half-day head of being served, Hmm. This was an interesting spin on pie baking.

When dinner was finished and it was time to serve dessert, the pie was presented before it was cut. Wow, it looked like a pastry out of Sunset.

Jim went on and on with compliments on the wonderful pie, and the excellent light flaky crust. I mentioned that my crusts were always like a Christmas surprise; I never knew just how my crusts would turn out even though I used the same recipe each time. I thought the compliments were a bit excessive, but I was really taken aback when Joyce turned to me and said, "The next time I make a pie on the weekend, I will call you and you can come over and watch me make pie crust and take notes."

"What? "That's really rude," I steamed to myself. I had merely made a comment; I hadn't asked for help!

However, I regained my presence of mind quickly and replied, "That is very nice of you. Call anytime." Ha. I was noncommittal. She would be too busy with her family and a full time job to want to spend half a day Saturday or Sunday with someone she hardly knew!

One Saturday morning about a month later, the phone rang. It was Joyce Ridley.

"Kay, I'm going to make pies after lunch. Would you like to come over and watch me make pie crust?"

Good grief, this woman wasn't going to let the piecrust lesson die! The chairman of the psyche committee in my head said, "Go do it and get it over with!"

"Thank you, Joyce, I love to.Liar, liar," I seethed.

Jim thought this was hilariously funny. I pointed out I was not going to be rude to her, and the sooner I got this over with, the better!

"And besides, dear, you thought her piecrust was so exquisite, I really have a goal to work toward to do as well, right?" I commented.

Joyce lived on the opposite side of the city, and it was a big inconvenience to get there, but I did. When I arrived, she had set out the measuring cups, the flour, and the shortening. What I thought would be a "hands on" lesson, was a lecture. It was a good thing I brought a pencil and paper. She performed all the tasks as she talked; I watched and took notes.

"You must carefully measure two cups of flour into the flour sifter; add one teaspoon of salt for a two crusted pie. With a pastry blender or two knives, cut in 2/3 cup of shortening. It must be at room temperature. When little balls the size of peas are formed from the blending, add just enough ice water to form a large ball of the flour/shortening mixture. You should never touch the pie crust with your hands," she continued

"Why?" I asked.

"Because the oils from your hands will make it tough. For a one-crusted pie, use one cup of flour and 1/3 cup of shortening, ½ teaspoon of salt."

"This will be interesting," the head committee chairman whispered to me. How is she going to roll it out and get it on the pie pan without touching it?

"Now you must tear a sheet of wax paper and carefully gather this soft dough into a ball. We will let this chill for about twenty minutes and then roll it out."

"Oh, joy", I thought. When it was time to roll out the piecrust, Joyce took a sharp knife and cut the chilled ball of dough exactly in half.

"Now you must tear sheets of wax paper, and carefully roll one half of the dough between the two sheets." This she did. She rolled a fairly round circle between the wax paper, peeled off the top paper, and expertly flipped the crust into the pie pan.

"Now you can carefully position the dough that is hanging over." I have prepared apples for the filling. You roll the top crust the same way, but you must fold it in half to place it on top of the filling. Then you must cut slits to let our the steam." You know that! The committee chairman exclaimed as all the instructions were given.

She scraped the bowl of filling into the pie shell, sealed up the edges of the pie, and the lesson was over! Yea. I graciously thanked her, and went home.

The next morning I decided to make a chocolate meringue pie as Jim had remarked that was his very favorite. Good! I could play it safe and make a single crusted pie with this new famous recipe. It went together ok, but I cheated and used my hands to gather the dough into a big ball. I made the chocolate pudding while the crust rested in the refrigerator. When I rolled it out I was surprised it turned out as well as it did. Wow, this was a cinch! My head committee agreed.

Finally the pie was all assembled, and the meringue baked. It was really a picture pie. Was I proud of it, or what? That evening I asked Jim if he would like a piece of the chocolate meringue pie I had baked using Joyce's crust recipe.

"No, he replied, "I really don't want any pie."

My head committee said, "Don't take that, after you've worked half a day on it."

With that, I picked up the pie, aimed and hit him in the face with it, turned, and walked out of the kitchen.

I have not made a chocolate meringue pie in 44 years.

I went to college in 1948 and was required to take a public speaking class. This is my favorite story of that wonderful, exciting year.

Cow College Comedians

Sally Wallis

Oklahoma A.& M. won the NCAA basketball championship in 1946 and again in 1947 so, many of us "stuck up city folks" who would normally attend upscale, Oklahoma University, decided to go to the "cow college" in Stillwater.

During my freshman year, I was required to take a public speaking class. It was made up of one other girl and twenty seven boys. I was not unhappy about these statistics since I liked boys very much. Toward the end of the semester, the instructor assigned us a demonstration speech, along with our oratory.

When my turn came, I approached the podium equipped with a makeup kit, complete with all of the beauty needs a girl could want. I called upon Hy Camp to join me on stage. He was a muscular, wrestling champ who was majoring in Animal Husbandry. This class clown had dark, wavy-hair and as usual a two day growth of beard. I placed him in a chair and got to work, while explaining that I was going to demonstrate the vast difference properly applied cosmetics can make to enhance a person's beauty.

I began applying makeup base to only the right side of his face, followed by a touch of pink to that cheek. Next the right eye received blue eye shadow and black mascara. Bright pink lipstick to right side of his lips, completed the glorious makeover.

Hysterical laughter from the audience warmed my heart, but poor Hy displayed a dismal look in both eyes. I commanded him to parade around the room to model the spectacular improvement with the right makeup. Several of his cowboy buddies tried to hug and kiss him.

I motioned Hy to be seated again and I completed my oratory by demonstrating how to remove makeup. I spread the glamorous half of his face generously with thick cold cream and handed him a box of Kleenex and instructed him to rub his face vigorously. As he obeyed me, the tissue fibers caught in his beard and he ended up with half his face covered with millions of tiny white fuzzes.

I took a bow to thunderous applause and a feeling of pride in my brilliant oratory. I was certain that I would receive an A from the instructor for my splendid lecture.

Only later, would this macho boy seek his revenge.

A week passed before it was Hy's turn. He ambled up to the podium with a long pointer stick and announced that his demonstration speech was to be on judging cattle. Smiling pleasantly, he commanded me to come forward. I humbly obeyed and he demanded I get down on all fours and crawl around the stage in front of him.

With professional arrogance, he explained that this was an unacceptable cow and defiantly no prize. Pointing at parts of me with the stick he explicitly noted that "she's too high in the hocks, flabby in the flanks and too big in the rump."

I couldn't hear the rest of Hy's disgusting oratory, do to the uproarious laughter of the class, including the instructor and even the other girl!

When Hy finished his rhetoric, I rushed from the room and never heard if he made an A, but I fervently hoped he made an F.

We built our home in a wooded area that is rich in wildlife. This piece is about the surprises, joys and lessons in tolerance that living in the woods brings.

Mister Tip Over

Darlene Fuentes

It was 10 p.m. in June. Frank and I had worked from 5 a.m. to 9:30 p.m. at the primary election polls.
Winding down, watching TV with the volume low, I could hear Frank snoring before the first commercial break. My eyelids were stating to get heavy, too, and the TV program was fading.
RATTLE, CRRRAASH! I jumped up off the couch and ran to the bedroom shaking Frank's shoulder. "Frank, Frank! Honey!" "I just heard a loud crashing noise. It came from downstairs." Frank bolted out of bed and slipped into his slippers.
"Where did you say the crash came from?"
"It sounded like it came from downstairs by the carport area!"
Drowsily Frank descended the back stairs, yelling, "Shoo, shoo. Get out of there! Go home. Shoo. Oh Shit. "
"Frank, what is it?"
"Oh, a BIG dog tipped over the trash container and has dragged trash all over down here!"
I was standing on the deck looking down at him. "Where is the dog now?"
"Oh, it ran off down by the deer feeding boxes."
Now the feed boxes were located about seventy feet from the carport. I was looking out to the area trying to see if I could spot the Big Dog. No luck, it was too dark, even with the motion lights activated.
After picking up the trash, frank came upstairs. "That's it, I picked up what I could see and set the trash container upright" "I'm going back to bed," Frank announced as he headed for bed.
Frank's head no sooner hit the pillow than I heard his heavy snore from the bedroom. I went back to watching the television. All was quiet. CRAAASH!

"Frank, that Big Dog came back. I heard the crashing noise again."

"Oh, all right!." He got out of bed and into his slippers again. Back down the stairs he shuffled, mumbling, "Shoo, shoo! Get out of here! Go home! Shoo, shoo."

Frank picked up what debris was near the trash container and set it upright. As he came back up the stairs he announced, "That's it, if it happens again, I'll pick it up in the morning!"

A moment later he was up and out the front door with a flashlight in hand looking around. Within minutes he was back. He walked through the house and out the back door this time onto the deck. He looked over the rail. Then quietly, as the back door opened, he whispered and motioned to me to come quick.

"Shh, be quiet." Quickly I walked to the deck and tiptoed to the railing. He flashed the light down. As he touched my shoulder, he whispered, "Look!" There in the bright beam of the flashlight was a Very Large Mahogany. . .dog? Standing on its hind legs with front paws in the air we were introduced to "Mr. Tip Over", our local black bear!

A "ticket-filled" Saturday was in store for me. Had I known, I would have stayed home!

Traffic Tickets

*Phyllis Wesbecker
(d. April 2003)*

It was Saturday and my husband was called to work that day. We had been invited to our friends, Beulah and Ross, who lived in Sherman Oaks. I decided to take our two children, Janice and Paul, and drive out to the valley. We lived in Lakewood and it was about a two-hour drive away. I did not drive much and I wasn't used to all that traffic. I decided to go up Lakewood Boulevard to Pasadena in order to miss some of the Los Angeles traffic.

Everything was fine until I got to El Monte. I was stopped at a stop sign waiting for people to cross the street. I think everyone from the outlying area had come to town that Saturday. As I waited, it seemed like forever. I finally eased ahead and slowly drove across the street. The first car I saw coming towards me was a police car. He motioned for me to pull over, and he turned around and stopped behind me. He asked me what I was doing. I replied, "Well, I waited for a long time and I thought it was my turn."

He said, "Lady, we don't take turns!" That was my first ticket.

We were almost to Sherman Oaks, and since we were running a little late, I was going along at a pretty good clip. Oh no! I looked in the rear-view mirror and there was a police car. He flashed his lights and I pulled over. He said, "Did you know you were going 20 miles over the speed limit?" I said, "No, officer, I didn't realize it." That was my second ticket.

We arrived at Beulah and Ross's and had a nice lunch and a good visit. I told them about my tickets and as I was leaving, Beulah said, "Don't drive too fast." I assured her we wouldn't and we started home.

I was supposed to get on the freeway at Rosemead, but I realized I passed it up. I turned to go back and lo and behold there was a police car! I stopped and when he came up to my car he said, "Lady, you just cut me off." I was almost in tears and explained that I was trying to get on that freeway. Just then a woman stopped her car behind the police car and approached us, very upset.

She asked the officer, "How do you get on that freeway?"

The officer threw up his hands and said, "Ladies, get back in your cars and follow me." He then took us onto the freeway. If it had not been for that woman stopping to ask directions, I would have had my third ticket in one day. Those were my first and last tickets.

I suppose every family has a treasure trove of favorite stories, little incidents that read like mini sitcoms Here are some memorable acts from our "Family Circus".

Family Circus

Mama Mia! That's Some Spicy Sauce!

Karen Romig

    Many years ago, when my parents were fairly newly married, my mother needed to spend a long, tiring day at a teacher's conference. My dad decided to surprise her when she got home with a batch of spareribs, using the hand-written barbecue sauce recipe they had wangled from their favorite chef. He hauled out the recipe card and proceeded to assemble and mix the ingredients- a dash-catsup, vinegar, salt, mustard, cayenne pepper he stopped cold. "Why do they put this stuff in such small containers?" He grumbled as he emptied the can and made a hurried trip to the store for more. Once back home, he added the rest of the cayenne along with the other ingredients, followed the heating instructions, and finally tasted it. His tongue blistered, his eyes bulged and watered, and his scalp started to lift off his head.
    Must be something wrong with that catsup! he thought, and wisely decided to abort the project awaiting an expert opinion. When at last the Expert Opinion arrived home tired and hungry, he welcomed her with the good news-bad news greeting that he had whipped up

some barbecue sauce, but that there seemed to be something wrong with it.

One very small taste confirmed that there was indeed something amiss! What did you put in it?" she asked as soon as her tongue returned to near normal.

"Why, I followed the directions exactly!" retorted my dad, defensively. "I CAN read, you know!"

"Well, just humor me and read them back to me" cajoled Mother.

Daddy proceeded matter-of-factly to repeat the recipe: "a half-cup catsup, a quarter-cup vinegar, a tablespoon mustard, twelve teaspoons cayenne..."

"Uh, dear," my mother interrupted, struggling to contain herself, "did you by any chance notice that little diagonal line between the one and the two?" It was the sort of question that didn't really require an answer.

All was not lost with the batch of bastardized barbecue sauce. For years after that they added just a pinch of it to a mix of catsup and vinegar and found it to be quite tasty. And who knows? Maybe he was ahead of his time! My father may have invented the world's first quick 'n easy spicy seasoning mix. If only he had sold it to Schilling or McCormick, he might have made a mint!

Drop Kick

Karen Romig

My mother was a great cook, but a bit of a klutz in the kitchen. She was constantly dropping a bowl or glass, with or without spillable contents. More often than not the item proved how breakable it was upon hitting the linoleum.

One evening as my dad stood watching, she dropped and broke a favorite glass dish.

"You know, Ruth," he said in his best advisory voice, "If you'd stick out your foot as soon as you drop something, you might deflect the fall and save the china."

That very evening while fixing supper, she picked up a serving bowl with slightly buttery hands and, you guessed it, started it on a fast journey south. This time, however, she remembered Daddy's sage advice. Unfortunately, her timing was a little off. As soon as the bowl hit the floor, as yet unharmed, her foot shot out, sending the bowl flying to the far wall where it immediately became history. My dad was impressed, and told her she had missed her calling. Sadly, however, there were no women's football or soccer teams anywhere in the country at that time....

Name That Tuna

Karen Romig

My mother and her best friend, Ena, were seated next to each other at a catered luncheon.

Mother was deathly allergic to shrimp, and her face fell when she saw that the entrée was a delicious-looking, suspicious-looking salad. As the waitress served her plate and moved on, Mother leaned over and whispered to Ena "take a taste and nod if it's shrimp."

Ena did as instructed, and after a moment, gravely nodded and proceeded to eat her lunch with great relish. Mother surreptitiously slid her untouched plate over to Ena in exchange for Ena's empty one. On the way home in a car full of fellow diners, one of the women remarked, "Wasn't that a simply delicious tuna salad?" This could have been the end of a beautiful friendship, but it wasn't, nor is it the end of the story.

Not too long after that, Ena became pregnant with her first baby. She had a boy's name all picked out, but was at a loss for a suitable and original name for a girl.

"How about Stephanie Dale? Mr. Ena produced a bouncing baby girl and promptly named her Stephanie Dale. Some months later the two of them and some other friends were chatting about babies in general and names in particular.

"How on earth did you come up with such a beautiful name as Stephanie?" Ena asked Mother.

To Ena's utter horror, my mother admitted in a voice that carried to the crowd that Stephanie Dale was the evil, warped protagonist in a lurid novel that was selling like hotcakes in town.

Moral: Enemies are no problem; it's your best friends you have to watch out for!

Well-Suited

Karen Romig

This one's on me: During my senior year of high school I managed to land a plum of a job - working after school and Saturday in the local clinic. One slow afternoon in late spring, the other two clinic aides and I were comparing notes on wardrobe needs.

"I really need a new swimsuit.", I wailed. "But there's no way I can afford the one I want, and I wouldn't be caught dead in the affordable ones."

A patient came in then and we went back to work. A short while later, Dr. Dasler, the optometrist in the group, approached me.

"I understand you need a new swimsuit, Karen", he said, "and I just want you to know that I would personally be delighted, on behalf of the clinic, to buy you the swimsuit of your choice."

I was incredulous.

"Do you really mean it?" I gasped, certain I hadn't heard him correctly.

Wow! What a work perk!

"Certainly!" he replied. "Any style, any color, although I personally favor red or pink. Price is no object." After a pregnant pause, he added

"There's just one minor detail: After you purchase it, I'd like you to take it to Mrs. Hennemen, the dressmaker."

With a sweep of his hand in the direction of my bust line, he said

"I want her to embroider in big block letters right there, "Eyes Examined." He paused for effect - "and across the back", pointing to my derriere, "I'd like it to read "Glasses Fitted".

III. Elephants On Parade

Voices of Vanity

Today's Dear Abby column published an item from a young lady upset because her "perfect wedding" was going to be spoiled.

The Perfect Wedding
Bee Mandell

Maria was upset. She had planned her "perfect wedding". Now her future
Sister-in law Rosa had decided to get married. She planned to have her wedding one-month before Maria's. Many out of town relatives would not be able to afford both weddings. Would they go to Rosa's because it was first?

A wedding is not a performance planned for the largest audience possible. It is an expression of love between two people to be shared by those relatives and friends who find it convenient to attend.

If Maria starts her marriage as a competition with her sister-in-law it is doomed.

I've read many items in Dear Abby and Ann Landers, and I hear many brides- to- be fussing about trying to create the "perfect wedding." Many don't want children attending. Children are a result of love. Yes, they do make noise. But it's a noise of love. Uncle Butch might get drunk. Just have a couple of strong young men to escort him out if he becomes a problem. That's life.

You don't want your crabby old aunt? She can't spoil anything unless you let her. Don't be embarrassed by your strange relatives. You can't choose relatives. You are not responsible for them. Now your friends are something else. You chose them. If anyone wants to miss the wedding because of an ongoing feud that's his or her problem, not yours.

Let me tell you about my wedding. It was a small wedding, about 50 people, one my parents could easily afford. We reserved the local temple. The local Rabbi officiated. My mother and I made the food for the buffet table and hired a couple of friends to take care of it for the reception. I made my own wedding dress. Friends shared flowers from their gardens. The wedding pictures were taken by a couple of amateur photographer friends. A friend sang "Always". My bridesmaids wore their own formals. So they didn't match.

No one was left with a hefty debt. All set for a happy, relaxed wedding.

The Rabbi performed a beautiful ceremony with prayers for a long happy, loving marriage.

When a toddler started to cry during the ceremony he stopped for a couple of minutes for the mom to take the little one out to the lobby. A couple of people coughed. There was a slight pause. No big deal-- that's life.

A Rabbi wears a tallis when performing a religious ceremony. It's a beautiful long white scarf with symbolic embroidery.

When the ceremony came to "you may kiss the bride." Lou swung his arms out and cuddled me close to him for the kiss, a long delicious one. We didn't know that he had caught the Rabbi's tallis pulling him forward and down for the length of that kiss. When he was released he stood up laughing. A temple full of people were applauding and laughing. Was anyone upset? Not at all! It was a moment of joy. Part of the joy of a " perfect wedding." We've been married over 50 years. What do you think?

To Begin Again

Ariel Edmundson

I send a prayer
Through time and space
Yearning for another place
To a distant star
To a place afar
Longing to be where you are
What I wouldn't give
To begin again
This time to taste the wine
And not waste precious time
Open every secret door
Not hesitate as before
Suddenly one day Spring is gone
As tide and time move on

This was written partly to honor my most faithful friend, and partly for my children's benefit. They all know Laurie, but perhaps they do not know the long history we have shared.

First Love

Karen Romig

Laurie entered my life in the fall of 1941, and it was love at first sight. He neither knew nor noticed me, but it didn't matter--- I was deeply, passionately entranced with this new classmate - as deeply passionate as a fourth-grader is likely to get. He had two outstanding characteristics that set him far above the other boys in my immediate world. First of all, his name-- in a town full of Johnsons, Petersons, Knutsons and Nelsons, a name like "Laurie Porter" had a magical aura. "He has such a cityish name!" I sighed to my mother that first day after school. Even more important than that, he looked like Roy Rogers - or at least how I was sure Roy Rogers had looked when he was nine years old. He had those same crinkly eyes. He was beautiful! Unfortunately he didn't return my adoration that first year. He was madly, passionately in love, first with Marilyn, who was really good at marbles and Red Rover, and then with Bonnie, who could sing and was teacher's pet. Most of the other boys felt the same way at the same time for the same reasons.

In fifth grade, however, I was the star, and it was Laurie's turn for purple passion. He wrote me love notes and passed them to my friend Loretta in the next row to pass to me in the row on the other side of her. One day the teacher intercepted a particularly syrupy epistle and read it aloud to the class. I tried to crawl under my desk. Laurie stayed home from school for two days until his mother found out what had made him sick and forcibly effected his recovery and return to class. Both of our mothers were teachers and good acquaintances of Miss Shafer, but, unknown to us, let her know in no uncertain terms that they thought her treatment of the situation was a bit harsh and high-handed not that either of them approved of the note passing, of course. Still, it was nice to know they didn't consider it a capital crime.

Laurie lived on a farm about three miles out of town. That summer, whenever I could con a girlfriend into taking a bike ride with me, we'd somehow find ourselves riding past the Porter farm. We never went in, of course - didn't even stop, even if Laurie happened to be out in the field. I pretended to be oblivious to the fact that we were in the vicinity of his home. If cornered, I was prepared to claim that I just wanted to see his dog-I forgot to mention Laurie's third attribute - a dog that looked like Lassie! His name was Zar.

His nose was more pointed than Lassie's, and that bothered me a bit, but from the back he was the spitting image of the movie star

I'll never forget our first kiss. It was in the park by the bandstand. It was a full-on-the mouth kiss, not just a peck on the cheek like I had hastily received from a couple of the other boys, probably on a dare. No, this was full contact, although as I remember no other parts of our bodies were involved, not even fervent handholding. I put myself to sleep thinking about that kiss for months afterward, reliving that ten seconds over and over and feeling all tingly at the memory.

Our romance continued at about that pace for the next two years, although I branched out a bit and allowed other boys to write me notes and walk me home --- I was nothing if not thoroughly democratic even then. But Laurie remained steadfast and resolute and loved only me.

And then, in the summer between 7th and 8th grades, the Porters moved to Texas, a world away from Wisconsin! Poor Laurie was devastated - a darn yankee (that's what he said he was -- he wasn't allowed to say the swear word) in the midst of a bunch of "suthuhnahs" who talked funny. He was lonely and miserable and wrote every day; I tried to answer at least once a week. Just about the time my interest in maintaining a steady communication began to wane, Laurie got to go to a Boy Scout jamboree in France. My enthusiasm was instantly renewed! Letters from France! Oh, Boy! I hounded the mailbox, waiting for letters with foreign stamps. They arrived regularly, and I was transported and enchanted by the comings and goings of what I now considered my dearest friend and international bon vivant. He sent me a tiny bottle of Channel Number 5, which I treasured and swore I would keep forever and ever.

The Porters returned to Wisconsin a couple of years later, but things had changed considerably. Laurie had affected a Texas drawl, which I thought was cute at first, but it became a real problem for me. We were cast in a play together, and during our first rehearsal, the rest of the cast broke into peals of laughter when I responded to one of his lines in an unconscious but perfect imitation of his Texicanese. He also wore cowboy boots. That was embarrassing they were noisy and none of the other boys had them. Meanwhile, I had several other semi-steady boyfriends to occupy my time, and Laurie had one crush after another through high school. Now and then we'd get together and discuss our current love interests, often amounting to my giving him advice on getting over his frequently broken heart.

Years passed, during which each of us went to college, got married and raised families. Laurie never left our home town; in fact, he stayed on the family farm where he grew up. I was all over the place. Yet, no matter where I lived, married or not, I'd get occasional letters, cards and packages signed "jus' me. The postmark was rarely from Amery, so for a long time I didn't have a clue as to "jus' me's" identity. When I discovered the source, I realized that what they say must be true: Men never forget their First Loves. The weird and wonderful thing is, it's been sixty years, and he still thinks I wear a halo and wings. Every woman should be somebody's first love - someone who doesn't see the crow's feet and cottage cheese thighs and remembers only the good times of long-past days. For a few moments, at least, it's possible to trade Alzheimer's for adolescence and return to puberty and pigtails. For Valentine's Day he sent a pair of talking Kissy Bears. It said "jes' me" on the package, so I guess I'll call them "Jess" and "Mimi" And one of these days I'm going to look for that bottle of Chanel Number 5 from France; I'm sure it's around here somewhere, maybe in the box full of fifth grade love notes.

We often find ourselves worlds apart from where we would like to be. This poem suggests you reach past your dreams and touch that someone. Life is so much more than wishing.

If Only

Roger E. Honzik

I'd be captured
by the phrases
I would love to hear you say,
if only I could hear them
if only you would speak.

But I drift
within my daydreams
and our worlds may never touch
words remain unspoken
my dreams are often thus.

I first met my husband when I was an Arthur Murray dance teacher. Later I studied briefly with Martha Graham, two exciting times in my young life The rhythm of dance equated with the rhythm of my life, thus "Metaphorically Speaking" had to be written.

Metaphorically Speaking
Alison K. Paolini

Together we have danced through the years.
Sometimes in the form of the Fox Trot,
In tune and at peace.
Sometimes we have moved to the Viennese Waltz,
Sweeping and elegant.
Other times we breathed the sultry beat of the Rumba,
Rhythmic and warm..
There were days filled with the timing of the Cha Cha,
Representing light spirits and mutual enjoyment.
Can you remember the days of the tango
Filled with fire and excitement? Time has passed.
Not without the Lindy,
The tossing away and
The pulling together.
A parallel to life and its patterns.

We have danced
For many years, in sickness and in health,
Through all manner of experiences
We shared.
We grow old together, still dancing,
Seldom the Rhumba, or the Tango.
Infrequently the Cha Cha or the Lindy.
We still have it in us to do a bit of the Waltz or Fox Trot.
Hey mister D. J. give it to us on the slow side.
We have more time to dance together.

Missouri Day In Fowler, Colorado

Vesta Steinacker

Every year, toward the end of summer, there was a day set aside from work to go the Fowler Park picnic. Folks would visit and there was a carnival for kids with a Ferris wheel, a merry-go-round and swing rides. It was a time for fun! At night there would be foot stomping music, a hoedown with guitars, fiddles, bass fiddles and piano.

Every one from miles around came and I always looked forward to going. Oh, I'd save my money from the farm work so I could enjoy the rides, and oh, how I loved that carnival atmosphere with the music and the games. Especially, I loved the cotton candy.

The year I'm reflecting on is 1949 and I am fifteen. The day of the picnic is August 3rd. Loise Martin, Doris Lee Mock and I had thought of nothing else for weeks except going to the picnic. Now Loise *talked* of nothing other than Bobbie Kidders from L.A. - as she called Los Angeles, California.

She had his name written over and over on everything. My mama said she was boy-crazy, whatever that meant. She told Doris Lee and me so many stories and now we were to meet this Bobby, his cousin, Harlan, and the buddy he had with him from L. A., when they got off work at the farm.

We were three young, giggling, silly girls standing at the appointed spot in front of the Ferris Wheel. Waiting with eager anticipation to meet Loise's boy friend, which we knew all about, we thought! I can still see those three guys walking toward us three giggly girls and again know the excitement I felt in Loise as she waited for her dream boy.

Never will I forget what happened next. I didn't even know this side of me. Loise was saying, "this is Bobby, and, Bobby, these are my friends", and instantly as he looked at me, I swear I never felt such a feeling.

What was it? An instant attraction, a spark between us? I saw those blue eyes, dimples and a grin, a devilish grin, as he reached for my hand and said, "Ride the Ferris Wheel with me."

Before I thought, I was running with him for the waiting seat, but not before I saw Loise's look of shock, hurt and disappointment all rolled into one.

Away I went with that Bobby, on that wheel, up, up into the air in more ways than one. There, far below, like in another world, stood the group; then, with us at the top, the engine broke down.

I felt, "Oh! What am I doing to Loise? "

"This is awful."I told this handsome guy. "What about your girl friend, Loise, you are to dance the night away with?"

He just laughed and rocked, grinned devilishly again as he rocked and rocked the seat, scaring me half to death.

"Why" he replied, "Loise, is my friend, and while we were talking on the way to my mom's the other night, she asked me to bring Harlan and Junior, and meet you all at the Ferris Wheel. And," he added for good measure, "I don't dance."

He kept teasing, rocking and flirting, saying, "Come on, go to the movies with me."

"No." I said, more weakly each time, as he teased and rocked harder. High above the world below I loved every second, yet I was also scared.

He instructed me, "When we get off, take my hand and let's run and find my mom where she is playing the piano for a dance. I will let her know we are going to the movies."

I attempted, very weakly, to make an excuse. What will Lois do, or what will my dad do to me when I get home?

Confidently, he replied,"Don't worry. I'll take good care of you."

I grabbed his hand as we jumped off the seat when our turn came. We took off running. We had a *running adventure* for forty-eight years, as there was never a dull moment from that night on with Bobby Kidder, who captured my heart and with whom I had three precious kids. He certainly knew what he wanted in life, went after it, and captured it. As he would have said: "Hook, line and sinker."

As a bystander among the lives of people, I look back with shame at the Holocaust. As a child what might I have done to ease the burden of so many? At least I can remember, never to forget.

Remembered

Roger E. Honzik

Clutched by views too sad for me
That haggard face of misery
Of children lost so willfully
Along life's break from sanity.
Oh! Bitter, grim and lowly task
To write the shame I feel at last
For all the children of that past
As they were smitten to the last.
Those unremembered names and souls
For bells of grace which did not toll
Still wander thru those lands of old
In search of oneness with their fold.
Yet tulips sway for them in spring
And morning birds will ever sing.

Why I Ride A Motorcycle
Ellen Eagar

My husband, Joe, had ridden a bike during his younger days delivering flowers for a florist and now he decided to purchase a new one. He bought a 750HP Motto Guzzi, which is an Italian bike, no chains and no noise. It had two carburetors, two exhaust pipes and a drive shaft, which made it very quiet. We began riding double around the local country and had a great time. However, he never wanted to take me on a long trip, as he felt uncomfortable. So, when he went on a long trip I stayed home.

In the motorcycle world, if you are left at home by your mate, you become known as the motorcycle widow and this I did not want, so at his suggestion, and after giving it some thought, I decided to have a bike of my own. But how was I going to learn how to ride the thing? We both worked five days a week and his work was shift work so there were times when we saw very little of each other. But he looked and soon came up with a 175HP Honda. It was very quiet for its size as it had been built for a street model in Japan and it, too, had two carburetors, two exhaust pipes and a drive line.

We brought it home and Joe set it up in the backyard on its center stand, which was a most unusual feature for a small bike. By doing this, the rear wheel was off the ground. He showed me how to start it, shift the gears, use the clutch and brake and then told me to get on. I did and it did not take me too long to ride the bike sitting on one spot. I started it, shifted gears, used the clutch and brakes and did everything you would do while riding it on the road, but I sat in one spot. I did this whenever I had time after work. When Joe was home, he would put it down for me to ride around our circular drive and he would throw things out in front of me so that I would have to miss them.

It did not take too long for me to begin to feel comfortable, so I donned my boots, gloves and helmet and we would go out on the road to get acquainted with traffic. We went nowhere without full protection.

I rode this little bike locally for quite a while and finally Joe said it was time for a bigger bike and we bought one so that I could go on the long trips with him.

Time seems to be the most precious gift we have, yet it is often wasted as though each of us has an endless supply. It is sad that we sometimes use time so unwisely.

Moments

Roger E Honzik

There's a spirit in the moment, guard it well.
For within the trackless hollows we call time,
There's but one, a moment's token blessed as now
Which is here and then is swept upon the winds.

Use well these precious jewels as they come.
Cast them not as worthless sand upon the shore.
Return a smile, touch a hand and be of love.
For the store of your sweet moments slips away.

Make no hoard of unused moments, to be saved.
They will be the timeless taunting to your waste.
Be at ease with life and spread your moments forth,
In full measure place them well and be at ease.
For all of life, which craves your moments,
waits for you.

In the year 1957 I attended college in Indiana, while my steady got caught up in the draft and eventually was stationed in Missouri. We seldom saw one another, and one Valentines day I received one dozen red roses, some of which I eventually pressed in a poetry book.

Love Then, Love Now

Alison K. Paolini

A rose petal, preserved by time and poetic pressure,
Fluttered to the ground as she opened the long neglected book.
The years had passed with occasional visits to the yellowed pages
Which embraced this and other petals.
Emily, T.S., Robert, D.H. ... all and more,
Were calling to be read.
But memories rose to the surface ....

She held one lovely preserved remnant of a long ago bouquet.
The petal felt slippery, satiny, soft, like old thoughts.
The color so true, the color so deep,
Brought visions of the long ago bouquet.
Her eyes became deep and moist.
A softness settled around her,
As that long ago Valentine briefly flashed before her.

Love then ..
Love now ..
Lo those many years gone by.
She replaced the petal between the leaves of poetry ...
She looked across the bouquet upon the table,
To see the twinkle in his eye.
Love now.

This is the story of a U.S. military family being transferred to Asmara, Eritrea in 1966. Eritrea then was part of Ethiopia and His Imperial Majesty Haile Selassie was in power.

Welcome to Ethiopia

Carmen Jury

Bob was in the Navy and had completed two and a half years of shore duty in Greece. When it came time to transfer to our new duty assignment, airlines in the States were on strike, so we weren't able to take leave and visit our families in California. Instead we were on our way to Kagnew Station in Asmara, Ethiopia.

Kagnew Station was a United States military radio receiving and transmitting facility. Because of its high altitude and location close to the relatively interference-free equatorial belt, it had unique technical advantages as the African-Middle East element in the world wide system linking America with Europe, Asia, and the Western Hemisphere. Kagnew Station was a U.S. Army facility with a contingent of Navy communication personnel.

We flew from Athens on Ethiopian Airlines to Cairo then on to Asmara.

As the airplane circled around, we could see Asmara sitting on a high, barren plateau. We landed safely and entered the small airport terminal with our two year old son, David. Our sponsor was chief Harold Stone who welcomed Bob with a hardy handshake and a bottle of Kaopectate. As we started through customs Bob produced his Navy orders and surrendered then to a fine featured, black immigration official. There was some confusion. Several other officials were called over and a discussion in Tigrinya ensued. Not understanding a word, Bob and I stood by patiently and waited. Bob was taken to an office and I was ushered to a holding area. I sat there exhausted from travel, seven months pregnant, with a bulging torso and David playing at my feet.

Bob returned to tell me that they would not let me enter the country. The U.S. Army lists dependents on their servicemen's orders while the Navy did not. His orders read "ETC Robert E. Jury and no others," meaning no other servicemen. The Ethiopian officials were interpreting it literally as "NO OTHERS." While Bob returned to haggle, plea, and beg them to let me through immigration, my mind retraced a journey through a maze of airports...Cairo, Athens, Paris, New York and San Francisco. I visualized a nightmare trip back to the States with a toddler. Feeling abandoned and alone, I waited.

It seemed like an eternity before Bob returned. He grabbed his brief case, rummaged through our papers and seized our marriage certificate. With it in hand, he returned for another round of arguing. Finally he came back with a smile on his face. He had won! We were ushered through immigration. Our African adventure had begun.

In this poem I hope to remind the reader that nothing is forever in love and yet how fulfilling and wonderful it is.

Evening Themes

Roger E. Honzik

Midnight dancers' steps renew
In the ageless throbbing life of two
Who whirl forth in tempting view
Of naught but they who dance it too.
For midnight's theme was ever thus
And acted out by those in trust
Reclaimed the wondrous depths anew
A rapture danced with strains by two.
Bow you flower, hush the bird
That ne'er a scent nor song be heard
To steal their dream within the dance
Which paints its never lasting trance.
Rise with morning's songs and smells
Begotten dreams unquelled, retells
Of dancers locked in ageless dreams
Which ever plays these haunting themes.

As I hurriedly snapped gold loops into my ears, I thought of how I came to have pierced ears. It was not socially acceptable for young girls to wear pierced earrings in l952, and sterile conditions for the piercing procedure did not exist.

The Ear Piercing
Kay Hinerman

Two days had passed since my high school graduation. I had received many cards, letters, and gifts; but there was one gift that caused me a lot of indecision. The day my mother went to the nearby town to shop, I knew it was "now or never." You see the gift was a pair of lovely rhinestone earrings. The problem: they were for pierced ears, and my ears weren't pierced! Mom wasn't keen on pierced ears.

" If you want to wear earrings, why can't you wear clip on earrings for unpierced ears?" she said. I reply, "ALL my friends have pierced ears, I look stupid 'cause I don't have mine pierced." Mom dismissed the subject with "Well, we certainly don't have the money to have them pierced."

A neighbor pierced everyone's ears, including the ears of all my friends; however, my mother has long ago dubbed Virginia Dietrick as a "fast woman," and certainly not a desirable person to be around. Why? Virginia wears long nails painted red, smoked, chewed gum, and was "bone lazy" according to mom. Those traits were undesirable in a farmwoman. I know mom didn't want me to have Virginia do the ear piercing; however, she hadn't actually forbidden it.

The afternoon wore on; I longingly looked at the earrings. I made a decision to pay Virginia a visit.

When she answered the door, I almost lost my nerve. My palms are sweaty, I opened my mouth to speak and no words came out. I thrust the earrings at her, and croaked, "Will you pierce my ears?"

She fingered them with her long red lacquered nails as she popped her gum.

"Well, Kay, come in," she invites.

"Does your mother know you're doing this?"

"Oh yes," I replied, without looking at her.

She gave me a fishy look of disbelief, and led the way to her sewing machine. There she selected a long quilting needle, threaded it with linen thread, and went to find her cigarettes and matches.

She came back into the room puffing vigorously on a cigarette as she carried several ice cubes in a bowl. In her other hand was a lead pencil, a raw potato and a book of matches.

Virginia pulled out her sewing chair and told me to sit down. She deliberately put her freshly-lighted cigarette, smeared with a half inch imprint of lipstick, in a cigarette-butt-laden ashtray. Wow!. It hadn't been clean for awhile.

She roused me from my reverie with, "Are you sure you want to do this, Kay?"

"Oh, yes, please. The earrings were a graduation gift from Sally and Helen."

"OK, we'll begin. You must help me out here."

I held the ice cubes on my earlobes until they were numb with cold. When I couldn't feel a pinprick on my earlobe, Virginia took the pencil and marked a perfectly centered dot on each ear. She's performed this procedure many times I reassured myself as I tried to relax a bit.

With a sharp knife she cut the raw potato in half crosswise, lighted a match and burnt the needle. She told me to look at a certain spot on the opposite wall and to hold very still. I stared so hard at the wall; my eyes begin to water. With one quick motion she thrust the needle through my earlobe. She held the potato half behind my ear and caught the threaded needle. About an inch of thread was pulled through my ear. One ear was done; one to go. Well, that wasn't so bad, I tell myself. She repeated the procedure for the other ear, and she's done.

There was very little blood and no pain. Virginia cautioned me to dab my ears several times a day with cotton soaked in rubbing alcohol. "Also," she further instructed, "Return in a week and I'll show you how to put the earrings in."

I wasn't looking forward to my mother's return from town. I tried to complete all sorts of chores around the house my mother needed to have done as I waited for her return. Finally I heard the car in the driveway, and braced myself for what mom would say. She walked in with her arms full of shopping bags, and told me to get the rest from the car. After I had helped her put away the groceries, she noticed the bloody threads hanging from my ears.

"I see you paid a visit to Virginia's while I was gone."

This story has a moral "Pay attention to where you are going, especially if you get on a street car, or there may be serious consequences. I learned this in a very hard and dangerous way.

A Narrow Escape

Carol Jean Main

The year was 1942 in Los Angeles. His name was Lyle and he asked me to dance at the West Adams USO where I attended on a regular basis to do my bit for the War effort. To entertain the service men was Patriotic, after all. The fact that I was enjoying myself was beside the point.

We hadn't been dancing long before I knew he was fresh off a farm in Iowa, that his mother had died a few days before he was drafted, and that he was a very lonesome and saddened young man. But since my heart was already headed in another direction, though only I knew it, I tried to discourage Lyle when he asked to see me again. He wanted my phone number and address, but I said we couldn't give them out. But I did say that I'd be there at the next dance. Well, to my surprise, he showed up on my doorstep the next day. It seemed, our hostess had taken pity on him and had given him my address.

My folks liked him and didn't discourage him from coming again. In fact, Mom invited him to eat with us that night and Dad asked if he'd like to go with us up to Mt Wilson to see the observatory, Lyle readily accepted while I gave my Dad a frown and I hardly ate my supper. My family didn't know about my other fancy.

That Sunday we went to Mt Wilson and I was not very nice to Lyle, sitting as far as I could from him on the back seat and doing nothing to encourage his attention. because, realizing what a nice boy he was and that I wasn't going to fall in love with him, I didn't want to hurt him. But, then I did weaken and agreed to see a show with him the next Saturday night. We took the J streetcar downtown to Warner Bros. It was located on a corner and there was an Orange Julius to the left of the lobby. When we came out, I was tired and didn't remember where it was. This time it was on the right side. As we went out on the street there was a yellow streetcar and we ran and caught it, assuming it was the J car. We rode forever, it seemed, both of us getting sleepier each block. With lights on inside, I didn't see what was outside. All of a sudden, I realized, we were the only ones on the car beside the conductor. About that time, he called out, "We are almost to the car barns - you'll have to get off now."

I nearly died, knowing where the car barns were. Being new to the area, poor Lyle had trusted me.

We got off and found ourselves in the middle of the warehouse area. Not a light in sight, it was past midnight, Saturday night, no phones anywhere and no more cars. We began walking, back the way we had come, following the tracks. After several blocks, we heard the noise, coming from around the next corner. It was a gang of Pachucos, yelling, swearing and bottles clinking. They were a murdering bunch of hoodlums. My heart stopped, then began pounding like crazy. We were doomed - no place to hide. Then, just before they rounded the corner, we came upon a very small doorway, slightly indented. We slipped in and huddled together, praying they wouldn't turn and see us, knowing full well, Lyle would be killed and I'd wish I would be too.

The hoodlums didn't turn around. We waited until they were out of hearing and peeked out to be sure they were out of sight. Then we continued on our walk until we hit the A line and a streetcar came by. This car went within a mile of my house.

Having foolishly worn high heels, my feet were swollen and in great pain. Lyle didn't complain, and I kept apologizing for being so stupid and nearly getting him killed. We reached my home at 4:00 AM. My poor folks were so scared. I'd never been out that late before. Lyle was kind to me and forgave me. So, when he had to move on, I told him to let us know where he ended up. It was a little Island in the Pacific. He wrote to me and I answered his letters in a friendly manner, knowing he was still a lonely, homesick lad.

Two years went by and I became engaged to my love, when our hearts finally came together. But I didn't write that to Lyle. I couldn't, not while he was over there. So, sometime later, when he called me from LA and said he and his Dad were in town and could he come out to see me, my heart sank. But, not having the nerve to tell him over the phone that I was engaged, I let him come to our door. His father had stayed in the car. I showed him my ring, knowing I was hurting him and feeling just awful about it.

I never wanted him to care about me. He just did. He wished me happiness then turned away and took leave. I cried when he was gone.

Three years later, Dick and I were married and living in the Valley. Lyle went to our old home and saw my Grandma; he asked if I had married. Telling him yes, she gave him our address, saying we'd we glad to see him. He never came. I kept hoping he would with a wife; then, I wouldn't feel so guilty. But through the years, when he came into my thoughts, I said a prayer for his happiness.

Lessons are sometimes learned in the most unexpected ways.

Boarding School Days

Barbara Lang

Last May I attended my 50th Year Classmate Reunion at the Academy. I'm not sure why our school was referred to as the Academy rather than High School; perhaps because it was a co-ed parochial boarding school, and was founded in the early 1900's. The Academy ceased to be a boarding school ten years after our class graduated, and continues to operate as a day school. The old wood frame dormitories and Ad building had been torn down and replaced by contemporary modular classroom buildings. Our Reunion was held in the gymnasium, the only building still remaining from the good old days. There we gathered in groups, growing nostalgic, swapping memories and stories. Some of the hilarity of living in the old Dorm I had forgotten; or was it just selective memory?

We lived in a dormitory with 150 other girls in what must have seemed to our Dean to be one, huge, perpetual pajama party. Rules were there to bend, fun was to be had at all costs, and life was one big giggle. The enforced quiet study hall each evening from 7:30-9:30 became a challenge to see what one could get away with. Contraband radios came out from their hiding places in closets. We attempted sneak trips past the hall monitor to get downstairs to the showers in order to get a jump on 9:30 p.m. rush. Gatherings in rooms to eat peanut butter and jelly on bread and play a game of Rook, were doubly hazardous, since card games were forbidden.

When the 9:30 bell rang to announce the end of Quiet Study Time, the old dorm erupted, doors slamming, girls rushing to showers, or to line up at the telephone to call home. My roommate and I thought the polished hallways were great for a bowling game with oranges from the cafeteria. At 10:00 P.M. it was Lights Out; then life must continue by flashlight. It would be unthinkable to break our nightly routine of putting our hair up in pin curls, then polishing our white saddle shoes, while gossiping about who broke up with whom that day.

Usually a Dean in the Girl's Dorm would last one year or less. We had worn out several by my Sophomore year. And then came Mrs. Tate. It was obvious right from the start, that here was a no-nonsense woman. A formidable woman, Mrs. Tate stood tall and straight, we suspected with help from a corset. Her salt and pepper hair was tightly waved. Framed by horn rimmed glasses, her piercing gray eyes seemed to bore though to our souls. Whereas our former Dean had been sweet and motherly and easily reduced to tears, Mrs. Tate let us know that nothing would get by her. And we believed her. It was rumored, and later confirmed, that our new Dean's former occupation had been preceptress for a Girl's Detention Home. Of course that went over big. We were certain that she knew all, could see all, and had eyes in the back of her head. We were scared to death of her. She was secretly called "Old Ironsides".

Mrs. Tate had impossibly high standards, we thought. In our evening Dorm meetings (Worship) she lectured us on deportment, and the responsibilities of being Christian Young Ladies. "Boys will be boys", she would say, "But it's the young ladies who set the standards." We were admonished on the perils of going steady (not that any dating was allowed on our campus), and the evils of makeup, movies and other worldly indulgences. Girls who broke rules went through interrogation and cross-examination.

Some of the old fun traditions were no longer allowed. No one really understood why Mrs. Tate banned our Saturday night pajama parties, when we would line up mattresses on the floors, everyone sleeping together, singing, and being silly. It had been great fun.

The Dean solemnly explained that "Sin could creep in", and that we should sleep in our own beds. We weren't sure what to make of that.

Each morning Mrs. Tate stood as a sentinel in her office doorway, checking out each girl as she passed her on their way to classes. We imagined that those sharp and all-knowing-gray eyes checked us out from head to toe. Only a stupid person could expect to get away with wearing a bit of makeup or having bare legs. (Bobby socks were to be worn on school days, and nylon hosiery all day on the Lord's Day.)

About makeup, she liked to say to her girls: "Certainly, you may wear makeup, as long as your own mother can't tell you have it on." She could not be fooled, I soon found out.

I was in a crisis. I was due to board the bus for a choir trip in ten minutes and my last pair of nylons had a huge run. If I missed the performance, I would be in big trouble with Mr. Davis, the Director. Mr. Davis, to me, was right next to God in the order of people not to displease. In desperation, I would try that old trick used by clever women during WWII, when nylons were so scarce. With an eyebrow pencil and my roommate's help, I carefully drew a line down the back of each leg to simulate hose seams, then put on my choir robe, and hoping it would be long enough to cover my legs, ran down the stairs to the main floor. Mrs. Tate stood at her usual watch in her doorway.

Nonchalantly, I hurried past her, feeling her eyes bore through me; sure enough, my pseudo hose fooled her not. I was busted.

I was led to the dreaded office. Ashamed of my attempted deception, I cried and blubbered something about getting suspended from Choir for missing the trip. Mrs. Tate ignored my excuses, and began to speak about honesty, responsibility and procrastination. Procrastination? An unfamiliar word to me, I wondered how it fit here. How long", she asked, "Have you known that you were out of stockings? Since last week?"

I had to admit that was true. But I had forgotten until today, and besides, there hadn't been a town day to shop, and besides, I didn't have any money. She corrected me: "No, you waited until today to take care of it." The subject turned from stockings to school work. Did I goof-off during study periods, then have to study by flashlight later?

Did I wait until the last minute to study for exams, write book reports and themes? Reluctantly, I began to see the picture. I had a bad habit of flying by the seat of my pants, winging it in everything I did. Sometimes it worked; many times it didn't. No one had ever made me see this character flaw before. Finally, our little conversation came to an end, and Mrs. Tate seemed to actually smile a bit. She expressed confidence in me and my abilities, and to my amazement, she promised to speak with Mr. Davis about my unexcused choir absence.

I didn't know it then, but that experience became a defining moment for me. Would I never again slip into the old "do it later" mode? Hardly. I still struggle with that; but I know it for what it is..... procrastination. And I learned it from Old Ironsides.

Age brings wisdom. I passed up the opportunity to learn a skill, that would have served my better than the few "quick dollars" I made modeling.

Why I Never Learned to Type

Phyllis Wesbecher
(d. April 2003)

After my husband and I had been married about a year, he decided to take some evening classes at the college. He wanted me to sign up for something so we could attend together. Since I had never taken typing in school, I thought that would be useful and interesting.

The first night of classes, I was walking down the hall to my classroom when I was stopped by a gentleman who asked if I would be interested in modeling for his art class that evening. He explained that his model didn't show. I asked him what I'd have to do and he said, "Just sit on a chair on a platform in front of the class so thaey can draw your portrait." He said he would pay me five dollars an hour to sit there. At the time five dollars wasn't bad. I thought I'd rather made a little "mad" money that I could spend on anything I wanted than sit in typing class. I readily agreed.

It is hard to sit very still and not move at all. I had two small breaks but it was very tiring. After class, he asked if I'd come back next time. I hesitated until he said if I'd wear a bathing suit he'd pay me ten dollars! I agreed and when I told my husband, he said, "Just make sure you don't agree to model nude whatever price he will pay."

I modeled for that class several times, but he never asked me to model nude. I liked the money, but the job was boring. Later I wished I had learned to type. It would have lasted longer than the few dollars I earned!!

Have you ever been asked: What brief span of time in the past held the power to most shape your life.This answer, and the "historical" event took place in Stockton, California. 1948.

The World Turns in Five Minute Segments

Dawn McFarland

"Hi, Sunshine, what's good on your menu today?" asked the tall, lean young man perched on a stool in Red's Mecca - a bar and café combined.

"Well, Sailor, what about a double-decker burger with all the works? Instead of French Fries it comes with crisp, scrumptious Tator Tots. An exclusive only at Red's!"

I stood poised with pen over pad ready to write his order. Six foot, hazel eyes, with eye lashes I would have killed for, and the cutest dimple in his chin; I took it all in at a glance, then wrote him up for the special.

I was only a part time waitress at Red's, and worked at a nearby hospital in the billing department. I tried to look on my hours spent in a bar as helping out the owner, my friend. My strict upbringing would have allowed no reason for me to be there otherwise, and while I was friendly, I had learned to establish a certain distance between the clientele I served and me. Most of our customers were stationed at the nearby Rough and Ready Island Naval Base.

It would have been timely had I remembered to review all this right then, for I was being quickly and irresistibly drawn to my newest customer.

I took the order to the Seaman 1st class with the lean hungry look. Taking note of his ash brown wavy hair, I sighed, as many a girl would have loved to run her fingers through those curly locks. Business was slow at the moment and we engaged in lighthearted conversation. There was something different about this quiet boy from Iowa, he had a certain charisma seldom seen in one so young.

When he stood to go, he hesitated, then blurted out, "Would you go to the ship's dance with me next Friday night?" Oh no! Not again. I had turned so many of the guys down because I could not dance. I knew I really wanted to know this tall sailor better and even though my pulse raced at the thought, I murmured, "I am sorry, I don't dance."

"I will teach you," was his quick comeback, "is it a date?" I nodded weakly and he went whistling out the door. So much for keeping your distance from the customer, I thought.

Friday evening found me ready before seven. I spun my soft, sheer dress with its skirt falling in graceful swirls as I moved quickly around the kitchen at work. I had a fresh Camellia in my hair and my tummy was doing flip flops. Mac had agreed to pick me up at Red's where most of the naval men would meet their dates.

Seven-thirty came and went. "He must have missed the base bus," I mused, and continued waiting patiently, for another forty-five minutes, till I could no longer deny that I had definitely been stood up. My weekend was spoiled. But that was the end of him! Better to have learned right from the start that he was insensitive, thoughtless and irresponsible!

Several days later, I glanced up to see Mac walk in the door, seat himself at the bar, and order a drink. Never a very assertive person, I surprised myself by walking near to where he sat, raising my voice slightly, and speaking for all who listened, "Well look who's here. Would you care to offer an explanation for your absence last Friday night?"

You know how a whipped puppy looks at you? That was the expression on his face. Then he offered three simple words "I am sorry." Just that. The whole room was silent waiting to hear what I would say next. From the back the chef called out, "Order up!" in a tone that said, I better get down there right away. As I turned to go, Mac stood, hesitated just a moment, and then followed me.

"Will you go out with me after you get off?" he queried. I glanced at him aghast; what did he think I was? An air-headed doll so overcome with his charm that I could be tossed aside and forgotten, then picked up, dusted off, and tucked under his arm? All because he said, "I am sorry?!" Again our eyes met; why, I wondered, did he have to be so cute, so charming? I would be a fool to go. I did not answer and he returned to his bar stool.

When my shift ended, my way out took me behind the stool

where he sat. He had already had too much to drink, empty and full glasses sat before him. I stood there unnoticed. *Someone* had to look after this underage farm boy, I decided, so I pushed the glasses away, pulled him to his feet and out into the fresh evening air. I would walk him till he became sober, see him on the bus and safely back to his ship.

Somebody needed to.

In the five minutes it took for me to make this decision I had assumed the role of Caretaker for an alcoholic. A journey that led us into marriage, fragile happiness, tears, heartbreak, and an eventual separation of 16 years; as well as a close encounter with death - for him. A miraculous reunion gave us back every year plus an added ten percent.

In such short passages of time, lives and lifetimes are shaped.

IV.
Walking The Tightrope

Voices of War and Victory

The child that grew up in Amsterdam during the war years 1940-1945 carries images through THE WINDOW.

The Window

Hannie J. Voyles

Horror casts a shadow
that is forever mine
dressed in finest fashions
or dine with wine sublime
the shadows deeply echo
the sounds of a different time.
The sun sets in the window
orange bombs imbed
the hordes are slowly moving
toward the oven led
an entire civilization
alone cold and dead.
So tell it to the children
their eyes the size of fear
when the nights are screaming
they know that death was near.
Tell them of the horror
they know when it began.
Tell them of the horror
goosesteps as they ran
all those people going
to the place of death,
left----to grow so hollow
so lonely, so bereft.

Written for my children and grandchildren. This trip happened in such an incredible way that I was always to think of it as our miracle trip-taken just before our fiftieth wedding anniversary and just a year before my husband's death.

Our Miracle Trip - V. E. Day 1995
Florence Johanson

In May 1995, England was preparing for a big celebration to commemorate the anniversary of V. E. Day-the day that victory in Europe was to mark the beginning of the end of World War Two. The war had taken a devastating toll on that small island, turning it into a battleground where little children went to school each day with tiny gas masks packed next to their school lunches! Memories of that horrible time were still vivid in the minds of the British people and also in my husband's mind because he had been there. He had been there to fight and he had been there to celebrate victory!

That Art and I were to be a part of that English V. E. Day celebration 50 years later was something I never would have imagined and the whole experience still seems like a miracle to me!

Art had always dreamed of returning to England some day to locate the site of Great Ashfield, the airbase where he was stationed as a B17 pilot during World War Two. However, 40 years of working 12 to 14 hours a day in his own optical lab had left little time for travel, so the dream had to wait.

When Art retired, however, we quickly discovered that we couldn't balance our pocketbook and our trip plans so we lowered our sights and started to travel within our own country to places we had never been that were more accessible to us-places like Washington DC and New York City. They were wonderful trips but I still could not give up on Art's dream and I finally decided to put it into God's hands. If it were to be, He would have to make it happen!

One day, while we were traveling through Mobile, Alabama, we met an English couple who were staying in our motel. Art had spotted the woman on a little patch of lawn out in front of our room.

He said,"I have to go out and see what that strange lady is doing." It turned out that she was patiently trying to photograph a bird.

Eventually her husband and I joined them and two hours later we were still standing outside our room visiting. Fred and Margaret proved to be friendly and full of fun. Most amazing of all was the discovery that their home in England was near Art's old airbase!

Since we were both headed to New Orleans, Fred tried to book into our motel there. We were all disappointed to find it full so, after exchanging home addresses, we said our goodbyes and Art and I spent the morning of the next day in Bellingrath Gardens in Mobile. In the afternoon we drove through pouring rain and pulled into our motel toward dinnertime. Waiting for us inside the security gate were our new friends. Somehow Fred had wangled a room!

We had a wonderful time together in New Orleans and before we parted, each to return home, Fred took both my hands in his and said, "We want to make your English dream come true." Margaret gave me a warm hug and whispered in my ear that they wanted us to come to England and to stay in their home. They would help us find the old airfield!

Art and I left that encounter with our heads swimming but feeling as though we really could not take advantage of such a generous offer from people who were, after all, pretty much strangers to us. Back in California there were postcards from England waiting for us assuring us that we were welcome. For most of the next year we received phone calls, travel brochures and letters-all gently nudging us. Finally we looked at each other and said, "I think they really mean it!"

Plans began in earnest and, for the first time, we believed our dream was becoming a reality. INCREDIBLE! Through several unforeseen circumstances, such as an injury to both of my legs in a bicycle accident and pressing family matters, we found, purely coincidentally, that we would be in England at the very time of the V. E. Day festival. Our travel agent thought that it would bother us because of the crowds. We said that it would not interfere with our pleasure and gave it no more thought. CRAZY! Actually, it turned out to be the perfect time for our trip. Art had been in London on the original V. E. Day-in Piccadilly Circus--when the whole city went crazy. A time he was never to forget! Things could not have worked out more perfectly! A MIRACLE!

The trip was beyond our imaginings! We saw all the things I had read about in my history books and retraced Art's World War Two steps-rode the Tube to Piccadilly, looked around London, saw the queen and the Guard maneuvers in front of the palace as well.

I even spotted the queen driving by right in front of the ice cream shop while we were eating! I exclaimed to Art that I thought I had seen "Her Royal Highness" in the Rolls Royce that passed with a little flag flying from the hood ornament. Art thought I was getting pretty carried away but a nice British passerby heard him teasing me and stopped to assure me that I had indeed seen the queen!

The VE anniversary was commemorated, in part, by the lighting of bonfires across the British Isles. That Art and I observed a moment of silence as we ate dinner with fellow travelers in a small pub in Scotland. Then we donned party hats and blew horns passed out by the proprietor. After dinner, the bus driver took us to the top of a barren knoll where a bonfire was laid. As we watched the flames light the black, cold night sky, we all thought back to a time over fifty years ago when we were living in fear and uncertainty. How thankful we were when that time ended!

Yes, we did find that old airfield site. It was purely by chance that we got our first clue as to its location when one of Fred's neighbors started to chat with Art as he was taking his morning walk. Fred drove us to a pub in the vicinity where we discovered photos on the wall of some of the crews from Art's bomber squadron. An elderly gentleman having a drink at a table nearby overheard our inquiry as to the exact location of the airfield and gave directions! We drove over several country lanes onto an open, green field where remnants of stone buildings were still standing. There, Art and I got out and walked silently, hand in hand, over the grass. We each had our own memories. His were of taking off in his plane in "close formation" surrounded by fog so thick that he could barely see his own wing tips and only imagine where his neighbors were. Mine were of trying to imagine what HE was experiencing and worrying-always worrying. Fred and Margaret stayed quietly back at the car and we did not know until afterward that they were filming us with their video camera to preserve the memory.

Everywhere we went on buses, even on a side trip to Paris, people honored Art and thanked him for helping them win the war and liberate their countries. The young men wanted to shake his hand and tell him what a great debt they felt they owed him and all of those like him who had risked their lives on soil that was not their own.

As a surprise, one day, we were taken to a special memorial rose garden that had been erected in honor of the men in the 8th Air Force. Fred and Margaret were disappointed that the roses were not in bloom yet but the walled garden was beautiful and inscriptions on the plaques moving.

Art and I did not know, when we traveled to England, that it was to be our last trip together. He developed cancer and died in March of 1996, shortly after we celebrated our 50th wedding anniversary.

Fred and Margaret, our surprise friends, came to see me in May of '96. We had been planning their visit for a whole year and it was wonderful to be with them. They want me to come back to England now and perhaps I will-but it might be hard. Someday, though, I will be able to look at the video that Fred prepared as a surprise and brought to me after Art's death. There I know I will see a picture of two "not so young people" reliving a time long ago. There I know I will see, on film, the fulfillment of Art's dream trip. A miracle?

Part of my experiences during WW2 written for family members.

I Saw Bob Hope

Jim Laird

It was a typical December day in Hawaii. The last of our Battalion had arrived in Hawaii a couple of days before on the baby flat top "Citco Bay" from Kawjalein on our way home for our 30-day leave. It was early December 1945, and we were waiting for a ship to take us state side after 22 months overseas. We were a couple of days late to get a ride on the Aircraft Carrier "Saratoga" due to leave in the morning for San Francisco. She was loaded with about 5000 Servicemen heading home.

Leaving the base mess hall after lunch Ted and I walked past display booths depicting the different ways Americans celebrate the holiday seasons. I just had my 21st birthday and was feeling sorry for my self. I was moping around the barracks homesick for the first time since joining the Navy in 1943. My best friend Ted saw the notice Bob Hope would be doing a show nearby that evening. It was to be on a small stage set up in a nearby canyon. It sounded like a good diversion and might lift my spirits.

Just before dark, we headed in the direction of the show following others cutting across country going in the same direction. It was supposed to be less than a mile away over a nearby hill. It seemed like a lot longer than a mile when we topped the hill just at dark. There below us was a stage with a few bench seats just in front. Stage lights were on, and you could see that all the benches were full of people about the size of ants. The entire little bowl like canyon was filled with thousands of servicemen. We should have come earlier to have a better view. Some stood, but most sat on the ground.

They reached almost up to our feet. We sat on the grassy hillside and watched the "ants" crawl out on the stage below as the show began. The loudspeakers carried distant voices that could hardly be understood. We could tell that some of the "ants" were girls singing and dancing around on stage. After a bit Bob Hope came out. We could tell who it was by his actions and the few bits of his voice you could hear and the loud laughter from the audience when he gave his punch lines.

When the show was over, we stumbled through the dark guided by the glow of our base lights. There were a few beams from flashlights that belonged to people living on the base. The rest of us without flashlights stumbled along in the dark. Even if we owned one. I doubt we would have remembered to bring it. Yes, I am sure I saw Bob Hope that night so many years ago. The long walk helped me fall asleep to awake to a brighter tomorrow.

This is about a young girl's inner struggle when leaving home for the first time.

On the Brink 1

Zigrid Vidners

It was autumn of the year of 1939 and I was thirteen. In the spring of that year my father had retired from the army and our family had moved from Riga, the capital of Latvia, to the grandparent's farm. My father had helped them to buy it in order to farm there some day. Now that day had come for him. My brothers and I had already spent several summers there, first playing then working and growing up with all that there was.

Another summer was almost gone. The days were growing shorter. The cool breath of autumn was in the air in the mornings, though the days were still quite warm and mild. But the time of change was there for nature and also for me. Rows and rows of migrating birds cried their farewells, flying overhead, then disappeared over the forests. That time had come.

I too would be leaving soon. Usually this was an exciting time, full of joyful anticipation. To be back in the city, where so much happened, to see friends after the long summer, to be back in our regular life! But now I suddenly was not sure how to feel, because our regular life was not there anymore. Our home was now here, but this was not where I could stay. I had a lot more schooling to do and that had to be done in the city.

Since I had one more year to finish at the grade school, and it would not be wise to change schools at this point, mother had made arrangements with my friend Edith's mother for me to stay with them in Riga this last winter. I liked the thought of being together with Edith, but then again I would be away from my family. For the first time, I would be alone out in the world. What would that be like?

The autumn rains began. The big trees round the house wailed and groaned all through the nights. In the mornings the ground was covered with brown leaves and soon the trees were bare. Everything now looked so barren and sad.

As I sat in a room, watching the raindrops hitting against the window panes, I noticed some of them running down, then suddenly stopping, as if refusing to go any further, but, a moment later, they ran off anyway and disappeared behind the window frames.

Was it so with me also, as my departure time drew near? I wanted and at the same time did not want to go. And yet, I knew that I had to. It was decided. The thought of leaving the farm made me sad. Or was I sad about leaving this special summer behind me, this time of growing up? I did not know. I still had a lot of growing up to do.

The last Sunday morning arrived. Outside a white mist was enveloping everything and a strange kind of silence seemed to permeate all. Nothing moved, not even the smallest branch. The trees stood grey and lonesome in the mist, looking helplessly up to the colourless sky.

I needed to get outside to ease the heaviness that was in me. I needed to breathe the fresh, damp air, to be by myself. I put on the heavy jacket, the long boots and went out in the yard. I stood there and listened to the uncommon silence. Then I heard water dripping somewhere. Plop, plop, plop. Like tears that someone was crying, like a clock counting minutes of time that was passing by. Was it my time that was being counted out? I looked around, but there was no help anywhere. I slowly walked away across the empty fields. The summer was gone...It started to rain. At first a fine, misty rain, then it got thicker, soaking my hair and running down my face in little streams. It was time to go home.

By the afternoon the rain had stopped and it had become lighter. I was glad to see that, because the time had come for me to leave for the station. Dad had brought the cart to the front door and was putting my things in it. Everybody had come outside to say good-bye and wish me well. Our black dog, Murry, was rubbing himself against my legs, whining. I patted his head, he had been my good friend all through the summer. Then we were on our way.

The wheels rumbled on the uneven road as the horse trotted through the meadow and across the little bridge over the river. Why was I still sad? Why did I feel so strange? I was not leaving my home for ever?

"Surely I would come back," I argued with myself, but nothing helped. However by then, we were nearing the forest and, as I looked at the dark wall of firs and birches, their presence, as always, did something to me. I loved trees and I think their very sturdiness of surviving even the coldest winters gave me courage. Those green branches had a language of their own for me, and they told me not to worry and not to be afraid to go out into the big world, for they would be here, when I came back. They would be right here, waiting for me!

All of a sudden I felt free of my burdens, I lifted my eyes up to the tree tops where they met with the sky and knew that everything would be alright. I was at peace now. With a quiet smile to myself, I could say good-bye now to all that was here and to my first "big" summer.

This is a story of a fourteen year old girl's experiences during the last days of the Soviet Russian rule in Latvia.

On the Brink II

Zigrid Vidners

Almost a year had passed since the Soviet occupation of Latvia on June 17, 1940 - a year full of many changes and degradations of the Latvian people. Many had been arrested, taken for interrogations and many disappeared altogether. Fear was everywhere; nobody knew who would be next.

It was on the night of June 13 to June 14, 1941 that the dark clouds, which had been gathering over our country during the past year, were finally bursting. It was a night no Latvians will ever forget, for tens of thousands of people - young, old, sick and even mothers with babies were roused out of their beds in the middle of the night, given only a few minutes to prepare at gun point of surrounding armed men, then led to the open trucks outside where they had to join others, already waiting there with fear-altered faces. We did not know where they were taken. Only later did we learn that there had been rows and rows of cattle cars waiting in certain stations to take these doomed people to the Russian slave camps in the cold regions in Siberia.

I was living with my aunt and her family at the time in a smaller town in northern Latvia, attending the high school there, since my family had recently moved to live on a farm. The school year had just ended when all this happened. The evil forces were having a hay-day, and nobody knew what else might follow.

I had to get back to my family as soon as possible. My aunt told me to take all my belongings with me, for who knows, what more could happen. I packed and the next morning I was on the train to Riga. People sat withdrawn and silent, avoiding even to look at each other. I listened to the clanking rhythm of the train. Other times it had sounded like a joyful call to go forward, now the sound seemed more like the harsh pounding of a heavy hammer against bare steel. What more, what more will happen?

People were looking through the windows as the country side slid by, but they were stiff and frozen looks, suggesting that something else was going on behind their closed faces. They carried the hidden thoughts and worries which plagued everybody today, but could not be uttered. So much had happened in these days. So much hurt had been done to people. No one could stay unmoved by this, except the perpetrators, who were enjoying their revenge.

Now there were rumours that war had started, that Germans would come and Russians, knowing that they would have to leave, will want to hurry up to carry out their evil plans to deport more thousands and thousands of people to Siberia. Could that be true? Was there no way out?

We had arrived in Riga and I had to change trains. Luckily I did not have to wait long and got on the connecting train soon after. This train had open cars with an aisle in the middle and two-seaters and three-seaters at the sides, every two facing each other. Since my suitcase was so heavy, I sat down in the first two-seater compartment leaving my suitcase next to me in the aisle. No way could I lift it up to the luggage rack above!

The train was filling up quickly. Not much time was left before departing, but the seats opposite me were still empty. Suddenly the door opened, and two men appeared there in army uniforms with the high hats on their heads and sat down opposite me. I shuddered. Who were they? Militia?

My insides knotted up. I felt sick, but tried to keep my face straight and non caring. The train started to move. Now at least I could look out of the window; I did not have to look at these men and be scared. One of them was older and heavier, maybe in his forties, the other was younger and slimmer. Both were eying me with open pleasure and then smiling at each other like acknowledging something.

Their eyes turned to my suitcase. I glanced at it myself and saw that my name tag was right on top with my name and address showing. Why did I not think of taking it off? But now it was too late. The older guy was looking straight at it and even leaned forward to see it better, but the writing was facing me, so he leaned back again and just looked at me smiling.

Was this guy playing a cruel joke on me? Did he enjoy to see my fear? Or was this a pre-play for something more serious? A trembling went through my body, and at the same time my heart was beating wildly. What should I do, what should I do - the thought kept going through my mind again and again. They could pick me up here, and nobody would know about it. Should I get off at the next station? But the next train would be one day later. My family at home was waiting. They will worry if I don't arrive on this train. I looked out of the window, not seeing anything. Everything was flitting by, my thoughts did the same. I've got to keep cool! I've got to stay controlled, I told myself and so pretended to look for something in my handbag to appear calm and normal.

The men talked about something in a low voice. Then the older one got up and started to go down the aisle, but then he suddenly turned and stopped right behind me. I froze and clenched my teeth. Now! It's going to happen! But he just slowly bent down and read my name tag, slowly and with apparent relish. Then he returned to his seat, sat back comfortably and looked me fully in the face smiling, as if saying - aha! now I know who you are!

He really seemed to enjoy what he was doing and gave the other guy "an eye" as he did that.

I was almost beside myself, but there was nowhere to go. The train was running on. The fields and forests zipped by. The men glanced at the window occasionally, but mainly looked at me smirking or smiling provocatively and obviously enjoying making me uncomfortable. Especially the older one viewed me unashamedly again and again through half closed lids in his fat, round face. The younger one was less bold and later looked like he might be a bit sorry for the way they were treating me. I did not know if they were Russians or Latvians, but at this point it did not matter to me. In any case, they were in the opposite camp. I think this was the most torturous hour of my life. Then the train stopped at a larger station and, thank God, they got off! I was saved! The older one threw back one more smirk at me, then they were gone. What a relief! What utter relief! I could breathe again! I walked to the open window and looked out. The people were coming and going. Then I noticed a man in a grey cap walking alongside the train, looking at all the windows as if searching for somebody. Dad! My Dad! What was he doing here? And then he was at my window.

"My dear! Oh, my dear! I am so glad to see you!" he said with relief in his voice. " I did not know if I would or not. I was sent here with some others on government orders to cart gravel for some project. I may have to stay here several days. It will be so good to know that you are safely home. Tell them at home not to worry about me, if I have to stay here longer. Maybe I will have to leave the horse somewhere and go into the forest... You know what is happening... Greet everybody at home!"

The whistle sounded, the train started to chug out of the station, but Dad still walked beside it, looking at me so strangely with his blue-grey eyes. They were worried eyes.

"I'll see you soon!" he lifted his arm in greeting, or was it good-bye?

The train took on speed, but I was still holding out my hand to Dad, though the station was out of sight. It was so confusing. What was it that Dad said about going into the forest? And why was he sent here at this time? Were the same bad things happening here also?

Finally I was home, but the same stressful atmosphere was here too. The terrible, unbelievable news had travelled fast, even though many did not have telephones here. Who could do such things and why, because many of these were not rich, just ordinary people?

But there were some who rejoiced and were glad to have this revenge, to have the score evened out between the "haves" and the "have-nots", disregarding the fact that they were poor because they did not want to work, while others in the meantime had worked and made something for themselves.

One of these glad ones was Blackeye. He was one of the three persons to whom the communist government had awarded a portion of land, confiscated from us. We also had to give seed and animals to enable them to start their own farming as well as give rooms in our house. He was now walking around smiling in his beard as if saying:

"See? Now you will get it! Now you will get what you deserve! Just keep on trembling!"

Did he hope to enrich himself through this? It would work out just fine for him if we were taken out of the way, and then he could step in and be "the big boss" here. You could see the glee in his eyes already as he passed us by going across the yard.

What was happening here? True, we had the largest farm in the vicinity, and we had the new, big house. That meant that we were the bad people now, the enemies of the working class, because we had employed them. Now it was said that we had used them. But they were not slaves, they had looked for this work and had been paid for it. Rather we ourselves had been the slaves: Grandpa, Grandma and uncle August had never known anything else but hard work, and our family members had worked too.

Our parents had scrounged and saved all these years to have

money to pay for the farm. Even we children knew that we had to live frugally. But now we were made into criminals by the Russian regime, because we owned this farm! No, we didn't even own it anymore! That was heart rending for all of us.

After a few days, filled with worry and uncertainty, Dad arrived home. He and Mama talked a long time behind closed doors, then they talked also to Grandpa and Grandma.

The skies outside were grey. Dark clouds were rising over the forests, threatening rain. It felt like the whole of nature was rising up against what was happening here. In the evening Dad put on some warm clothing, his high boots and picked up his leather jacket. A silent hug to us all, then he took his hunting rifle and a small package of food Mama had packed for him. A short look at us all, then he walked silently through the veranda door out into the night.

Grandma turned away, wiping her eyes with the corner of her scarf.

"What a time," she was muttering to herself, "when people have to hide in the forest like animals..."

Grandpa too was sniffing under his nose and looked even more bent as he walked back to his room.

We did not question Mama and she did not say much. Her face looked hard as she told us that Dad had gone into the forest hiding, but we should not talk about it to anyone. There would be also others with him, she said, he would not be alone. It had been already arranged. The Russians were withdrawing now, because Germans were coming, that much was known now. We had to try to survive through these times.

"And we will survive" Mama said, hardening her face even more.

Part of my experiences during WW2 written for family members.

P.J. On the Rifle Range

Jim Laird

P.J. was a member of my platoon, #5 in the 141st Naval Construction Battalion during WW2. He was short with a strong stout build.

Having rickets as a baby he had very poor muscular coordination. P.J. wore very thick glasses that looked like the bottom of glass bottles. He was one of those who slipped through the cracks and was accepted into the service. We had a couple others like him. He was a very likeable 18 year old who tried very hard to please and we platoon members did all we could to help him stay in the service. After Boot camp at Camp Perry Virginia (next to old colonial Williamsburg that was off limits to sailors) we went to camp Endicot on Quonset Point Rhode Island for advanced training. Part of that training was learning to shoot rifles.

After a day spent with lectures and learning how to strip and assemble a rifle with your eyes closed, our next stop was the rifle range. The first rifle we learned to shoot was the M1 Carbine. One most of us would be issued before we shipped out. It is a very short light gun with a large ammunition clip and normally will fire a shot each time you pull the trigger. This day Company B divided one half on the firing line, the other the target butts. I was working the butts when P.J.s turn came to shoot. We were all determined to help P. J. get a passing score on his shooting tests.

His first shot hit on his neighbor's target.
The next one hit in the dirt in front of his target and sent a rock through the target. We lowered the target and marked the place the rock came through, raised the target and showed the hole as a hit.

We used a lot of rock holes (they are not round like a bullet hole) to give P.J. a pass on slow firing.

When he finished shooting from the prone position, we were a bit concerned, as we had not found one real bullet hole in his target.

When his turn came to do rapid fire from the standing position even his fellow shooter on the firing line were a bit apprehensive. With a full clip P. J. looked down his sights and pulled the trigger, his rifle started firing full automatic which it was not suppose to do. He was so startled he failed to take his finger off the trigger, with the gun still firing he turned around to ask the instructor what to do. Everyone along the firing line dropped to the ground.

Luck was still with him as the gun was pointed at the sky and ran out of ammunition just as he completed the turn. P.J. passed all his shooting requirements without ever firing another shot and he was never issued a firearm. He did his part by carrying ammunition for a machine gun crew.

"Most of all, we must go on". Your resignation, woven thru those dire words, caused me to search my soul for some peaceful thoughts that I could offer you with love and care.

Well

Roger E. Honzik

Only lately have I heard your words,
"Most of all, we must go on".

Never had I ever heard the "we".
Of course you meant, them
Those over there, the ones
I so easily over look, them too.

Now I question what you meant.
Of course "we must go on".

Yet you said much more to me.
You were saying, as you must go on
So must I. (So must we all)

My thoughts, my days
Are filled with words.
I scrape my soul bare
To find the words I need
To tell of whom I am
Where I am, what I feel.

All this with the hope
That others see within my words
That their paths could be
A nicer place to walk.

You also give me courage
To walk my path
To see past the sharp
And hurting stones.
Your courage helped me
See the beauty
That was always there.

And so my words must be,
Thank you so very much!

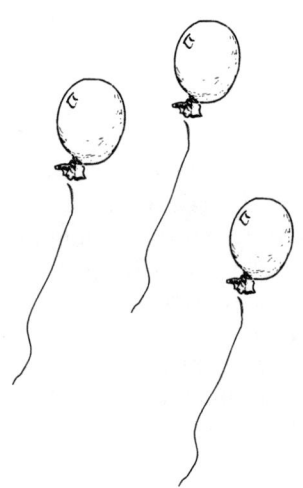

This story is a compilation of a few adventures experienced by a nine then twelve year-old American boy. These incidents took place in the Philippines during the Second World War. These events are his very own personal recollections.

A Desperate Prayer Answered

Frank H. Stagner

During the night of December 31, 1941, my family had barely escaped capture when the invading Japanese Army overran our location. My father had refused to surrender his family but instead led us to a secluded area in mountains east of the town of San Jose del Monte. Here, Father believed that we could safely sit out the war until massive reinforcements from America could arrive to relieve our embattled military. We felt very safe and secure in this remote mountainous jungle since the natives were very friendly and assisted us in any way they could.

This serene existence suddenly ended in the early morning of February 22, 1942, when we were confronted and captured by an enemy mop up patrol. My family was then marched across the nearby river to link up with the rest of the patrol and two captured US Army soldiers. Although having not been physically abused, I was aware of what could be expected from our captors. The two non-locals who had betrayed our locations to the Japanese may have been executed on the long march back to the patrol's headquarters. After about a forced four-hour march we eventually arrived in the town of Montalban.

On the morning of our third day of captivity, my family was brought out to the Town Plaza for public display. After enduring about four hours of the burning hot sun, we were then returned back to the schoolhouse. The patrol's senior officer later approached my father and apologized for the treatment given his family. "He explained that the Imperial Japanese Army had long been indoctrinated in the belief Americans were nothing more than cowards and crybabies. All one had to do was rough them up a bit and they would run home crying for their mothers. The Captain added, he was so impressed by we three boys' bravery and demeanor, he just had to advise the entire officer staff Americans were not going to be easy."

We, less the two soldiers, were later taken to Fort William McKinley by truck and again endured the same treatment. However, it was now very late in the afternoon and the sun seemed to be much hotter. Food or water had not been given us all day and I finally began feeling faint. My older brother Gordon, age twelve, desperately tried to keep me awake by nudging, and sometimes shaking and talking to me.

I must have fainted for the moving truck and cooling trade winds awakened me. As I wiped the cobwebs out of my mind, I recognized a structure the truck drove by as the Rizal Memorial Baseball Stadium. Still hungry and thirsty, my spirits were buoyed up when I realized we were now on a street named Vito Cruz. It is a short distance to the Tee intersection, and with a left turn on F.B. Harrison, we would be heading towards our Pasay home.

As the Japanese Army truck entered the intersection, the driver made a right turn onto Mabini away from the direction of our home. After a long block or two, a left turn was made and the truck was then parked at the curb behind the Magnolia Ice Cream plant. Hopes of having some delicious ice cream to ease my hunger were sorely dashed. The officer in charge of the guard detail stepped out of his staff car and began shouting orders to the two guards.

My family was pushed and ordered to stand up and face the sidewalk. After a few more pushes and shoves, the officer finally was satisfied with our positioning then quickly jumped back into his staff car. The truck was started up and proceeded to Admiral Dewey Boulevard where a right turn was made. The truck was driven very slowly this time as we were displayed to the populace enjoying the cooling trade winds and beautiful sunset over Manila Bay.

The large crowds grew silent as the truck slowly proceeded by them. I was able to observe the looks of fright and concerns of our situation. The journey continued all the way around the Luneta and back to our initial starting spot on the Boulevard. Again, the shouting and pushing ensued, as the officer was very displeased with our unbowed behavior. A second trip was began but by this time most of the crowds had suddenly vanished. A few of those remaining stood up and with eye contacts were silently telling me to hang in there. Some of these people were actually friends of Manila's large Stagner and Featherstone clans.

Darkness had now fallen, and our "showing" evidently was discontinued. We were then driven to the medieval Fort Santiago and it's once notorious prison. Our father was separated from us and taken to the dungeons below while Mother and we four children were herded into a ground floor cell. The cell had a small barred window and did not have any bedding or sanitary facilities. We had to sleep on the cold bare concrete floor and were supplied with only a small metal bucket for sanitation needs.

An inadequate but edible amount of food was provided three times a day. In addition, only one small gravy ladle of drinking water was allotted to each of us after the evening meals. The Military Police Officer charged with our confinement carefully watched the trustees dole out our daily rations. We boys strongly suspected the water bucket was our own rinsed out sanitation pail. My least personal discomfiture was that only one bath was allowed us during this entire period of captivity.

Mother made the mistake of complaining about the poor treatment we children had been receiving. The officer immediately charged into the cell and angrily began shouting directly in her face. He was so angry and livid, I thought he was going to beat her up. I cannot recall his exact words but the assertion was "the children were Prisoners of War and due to our very young ages, the Japanese Army was being generous and treating them with leniency."

I never could become accustomed to the horrible and blood curdling screams and shouts that originated from the nearby interrogation rooms. This horror would start in the afternoons and continue well into the late hours of the night. It was only after sleep came to me that I was able to shut out these terrible shouts and screams. One late afternoon, a muscularly built man dressed in gray shorts, tee shirt, and two toed tennis shoes suddenly appeared at the cell door. As he coldly scrutinized us, we boys noticed the chain with manacles, a club, and a coiled whip he was carrying. Without a word or change in his stoic expression, he turned and walked away.

The man's probable Japanese Army job description was not lost upon us. We now feared our uncertain guest status in this prison was about to end. Sleep now became even more difficult to attain this night. A thought of being executed, in the next day or two, was not something to casually dismiss. Gordon eased Lawrence's and my fears by suggesting we be brave and go to sleep. However, fears of how they were going to do it to us became very unnerving to my younger brother and me.

Gordon again tried to calm us down by explaining that we probably would be taken down and caged in the lowest dungeons. He sleepily continued the rising tides would flood the area and drown us. As an uneasy sleep began to overtake me, I kept praying for a rescue of any kind. I was firmly convinced our rescuers could only be the US Army. I had watched a number of old movies wherein the US Cavalry always arrived just in time. Most persons would have prayed to their Lord for deliverance but I desperately kept praying and praying that a tank supported Cavalry unit would come to our aid.

The next morning my apprehension increased when armed Military Policemen hustled us out of the cell and to an awaiting truck. A sense of fear enveloped me, as I did not know just what was in store for us. My fears quickly lessened when I observed prison trustees carrying our luggage towards the truck. I concluded the Japanese were not executing our personal property along with us. I heard a few cries of joy as our father was observed walking behind the procession. Dad appeared to have a difficult time walking and received needed assistance from a trustee. As he neared, signs of pain appeared on his face, including marks of physical abuse. After we all were aboard, counted, the truck was started, and we proceeded on a journey to another unknown destination.

The journey did not seem too long as the truck suddenly slowed and turned left into a large driveway. An armed soldier waved the driver on and the vehicle eventually stopped in front of a small masonry building. Groups of persons like our own selves stood around and cautiously observed us. The two MPs guarding us began shouting and gesturing for us to get down. A young American teenager stepped forward and began to assist my family to disembark. It was here, the University of Santo Tomas Campus, where we would be confined for the next thirty-five hard and repressive years. I was now twelve years old at the end of nineteen and forty-five.

On January 9, 1945 our armed forces finally returned and established a beachhead in Lingayen Gulf, located one hundred miles northwesterly of Manila. My biggest concern now was, would we all still be alive when our long awaited armed forces finally reached us? A large number of prisoners had since perished from diseases, starvation, and for some, savage beatings and/or execution. The expected mass murders of the remaining prisoners now began to form in my mind during this time. One day, my younger brother Lawrence and I decided to be early for evening roll call. We wanted to inquire of other boys if they knew of any new rumors. I also suspected something was brewing, as the demolition explosions were more intense this day. We both were so weak from starvation imposed by the cruel Japanese Army we could barely walk. None of my young friends cared to share any new rumors or else were simply afraid to discuss them in the open. Today's date was of no importance to us but suddenly, Saturday night, February 3, 1945, was the beginning of the most exciting and unforgettable period in my life.

As we stood around waiting for the adults and little children to appear, I distinctly heard what thought to be a low dull roar originating from the north. I quickly looked upward, expecting to see some of our fast and low flying twin engine attack bombers. However, the sound was simply too slow to have been from our Douglas A-20s or even the slower B-24 Liberators. The roar began to intensify as what ever was causing it entered the City of Manila.

My father rushed out to my brother and me, breathlessly inquiring if we had any idea what was causing this unfamiliar sound. The three of us then made way to the north corner of the Main Building. Dad then called out to persons lining the second and third floor windows for information. As dusk began falling over the city, a flight of about nine aircraft directly approached us from the north. These aircraft were at such a low altitude, I mistakenly believed they were about to strafe us. As they completed their pass over us, Lawrence and I identified them as the SBD Dauntless.

The thundering roar grew deafening as what ever was causing it was directly west of us. Heavy automatic and machine gun fire began erupting from the same general area. My father directed us back to our hut and to take cover underneath. A passing adult excitedly shouted to everyone what he had been listening to on a clandestine camp radio, I was now aware that units of our own military had broken through the enemy lines and was now in the city!

I grew very apprehensive as I listened to this cacophony eventually quiet down except for occasional outbreaks of gunfire. In my mind, I believed our troops had quit for the night and would be here in the morning. Lawrence and I quickly searched for anything that could be used to defend ourselves should the guards run amok and try to kill us all. Unable to find anything of use, we both just sat on the ground and quietly waited

Sounds of motorized equipment suddenly came to us from the front of our compound. After a few small booms and bursts of gunfire, the noise was now definitely within the University grounds. The growling and barking of powerful engines, with accompanying strange rumbling and clanking sounds were heard. I became totally beside myself when the ground under me suddenly began to shudder and shake. Outbursts of loud and joyous cheering then broke out in front of the Main Building.

My anxieties were eventually calmed when that same man again came by the hut and was shouting for all to hear. "The Boys are here, the Boys are here" was his ecstatic message. Lawrence and I stopped him and inquired what was causing all that noise and ground shaking. He jubilantly replied the sounds and shakings were the results of our own tanks maneuvering about the compound. As I watched him disappear into the darkness, I thought that I had seen him dancing away on air. In my own exuberant feelings of again being a free person, maybe I was indeed hallucinating.

Having survived the harsh and brutal treatment accorded us by the cruel and still unrepentant Japanese is an experience I shall never, ever forget. Through out my later maturing years, I could still recall these early wartime adventures and that incredible night of February 3, 1945.

While casually researching information for my failing attempts to record my youthful wartime experiences, it suddenly came to me that my desperate prayers for rescue had truly been answered! The Flying Column, whom had rescued us that unforgettable February night, had consisted of elements from the United States Army's First Cavalry Division supported by the Forty-fourth Tank Battalion. Both these two brave army units shall forever be revered and remembered by me for the rest of my life.

I wrote this story so that my daughter and her son will know what a different world I grew up in.

War Comes to Our Town

Laszlo Daroczi

I was six when a Russian soldier shot grandfather. We had moved in with mother's parents about a year before. I started first grade here in this small town in the western part of Hungary. Father was in the Army and was taken prisoner somewhere near Hamburg, Germany, in the closing days of World War II.

An old gypsy woman lived four doors up the street from us. She was the neighborhood fortuneteller. Mother often asked her to come over with her deck of fortune-telling cards. Each time the cards showed that father would be coming home soon. Eventually, she turned out to be right. Father did come home.

But now he was gone and I wasn't anxious to have him come home. We were free from his iron discipline and we made the most of it. When we weren't in school, we roamed all over the countryside eating berries and crab apples, and robbing birds' nests, and playing games.

Mother wasn't a disciplinarian. If we were quick enough, we could always dodge or run from a slap or a whack, and by the time we came back, the infraction was already forgotten.

You didn't dare run away from father. He had a system. He'd have you fetch a wooden spoon from the kitchen and you'd hold out your hand and he'd whack your palm as many times as the severity of the infraction called for. His parenting philosophy was to treat us to be like soldiers. Helen, the only girl out of six of us, was exempted and she took full advantage of it. She bossed us younger ones around mercilessly. I only liked her when she read to us about the adventures of three kittens.

When one of us boys cried, my father would say, "Don't cry! Soldiers don't cry!"

When we slouched with hands in pockets, he'd say,

"Stand up straight! Get your hands out of your pockets!" And most importantly, "Don't spit!"

I don't remember whether it was weeks or months after father left with the Army, that the war was getting close to us. School was now closed and the air raids came fast and furious. Sometimes the bombers came at night and sometimes they came twice in one day. When the siren sounded the alarm, we ran for the cellar. But first we had to open all the windows; otherwise the explosion of a close hit would shatter them.

The cellar was musty and dark and had water in it after a rain. Not long after the siren stopped wailing, you could hear the faint drone of the bombers way up. On clear days, you could see the tiny black dots falling from their bellies. We got pretty good at judging how far the bombs would fall. When you could actually hear their high pitch whine, it was time to hunker down. After the "all clear" sounded, we'd go looking for interesting pieces of shrapnel and lug them home. An oil refinery over to the east of us was hit. It burned for days and the night sky was dark red on the eastern horizon.

The railroad, which ran on the far side of the pasture behind our street, was also our playground. We'd lie on our stomachs next to the rail as the train rolled by and put coins and copper wires on the rail to watch them get flattened. Our noses were inches away from the clattering wheels. Also we'd walk on the rail for long stretches and graze on the berries along its banks.

One time a train was coasting down a slope bearing down on us. It was so quiet that by the time we heard it, it was so close we had to scramble to get out of the way. The problem was that both banks were covered with thick, prickly vines, and we wore only shorts and we were barefoot, as usual. We had no time for reflection and dived into the vines. Our sister, Helen, was with us this time and she just couldn't make up her mind to jump. She ran from side to side until we were all yelling, "Jump! Jump!" Finally, at the very last moment she jumped. It was a good thing for us and for our mother that she had no inkling of the scrapes we got into.

The railroad almost took a hit in one bombing raid. Two bombs fell this side of it and a third one just on the far side, much closer than the other two; but this last one was a dud. You could see the tail fins way down at the bottom of the shaft where it came to rest.

The two that exploded made huge craters, which later filled almost to the top with ground water.

That summer we used one of the craters as the community swimming pool. I learned to swim there. I remember the first time I got up the courage to dog paddle across the deep part in the middle to the other side. My brother Alex and a friend of his swam on either side of me.

On the far side of the railroad were rolling hills covered by patches of dense bushes. Here we often played games like hide-and-seek 'till dark. There was one area of steep cliffs where we found a foothold to inch along up to where the hawks made their nests. Inching our way back down was always more difficult than going up.

Still farther and over to the north was a fairly large creek. Our favorite swimming hole was just below the mill powered by a large water wheel. At the top of the water hole was a concrete channel, which slanted down into the swimming hole. It was slick with overgrown algae and it made a perfect slide. You had to be alert, though, because every now and then they opened up the floodgates up at the mill and you could easily be swept down stream. It happened to me once, and I yelled for help. My brother, Alex, yelled back to grab the willow branches dropping into the water on the far side. It worked.

Grandmother was short, skinny and humorless most of the time. She yelled at us a lot. She also yelled at grandfather, who seemed to pay little heed to her. At night, grandfather had to get up several times to relieve himself. He would tinkle and trickle into the chamber pot. Grandmother would cuss at him as he clambered over her.

Grandfather at seventy-seven was a large man with a powerful build. He had a handle bar mustache, which he kept waxed and also smoked a pipe with a lid on it. He was good-natured and was full of funny stories, which had us in stitches.

A lot of Grandfather's stories involved gypsies getting caught in the act of stealing chickens and the stories they made up to get out of their predicament. We'd beg him to tell this or that story again and again, and he always obliged. He was a saddle maker and had a special stool, which was also a bench. He'd grunt each time he pulled a stitch tight. Mother told us that when he was a young man, a circus had come to town and grandfather wrestled with the circus strong man. He put the strong man down, but he got a hernia from it.

The war was getting so close to our town now, that you could hear the rumble of the heavy artillery from the east. The German soldiers in the camp across the street were getting ready to pull out. Grandmother could speak German and she talked a German soldier who drove a truck into taking us with them toward Austria. The soldier did show up in the evening with the truck and we started to put our things on it. After a few minutes, he got a message on his radio, then ran back and threw our things off and took off.

The next day was quiet, eerily quiet. About mid-morning, we saw the first of a column of tanks inching up the road from the east. It had a red star on the side of it. Soon after that, it started.

The soldiers were going from door to door looking for booze, wristwatches, women, or whatever. They didn't take anything from us. They tasted some bottles on the shelves, spat the stuff on the floor and left. Others went though back yards and gardens with long, pointed poles, poking and probing. Where there was loose soil, they'd dig. They knew that people buried things in pits in their back yards and gardens to hide from the soldiers. They found the container of lard that grandfather buried in our garden. When they saw it was just lard, they left it.

One soldier with a red nose, dragged the sixteen-year-old girl who lived on our street into our house. He waived with his machine gun for everybody to get out. We all filed out into the yard and just stood around. After some time, Charlie and Alex, my oldest brothers who had been at the neighbor's house, came running home. Before anyone could say anything to them, they burst in the door. The girl was just pulling her skirt up. Some weeks later, she came over to talk to mother. She told her nothing had happened.

Some soldiers found a shed with several bicycles hidden. They were drinking by now from the caches they'd found, and tried riding the bikes. They were having a great time, clowning around and falling off the bikes. They ended up smashing them all.

The soldiers didn't harm the two ladies who lived next door to us. They were mother and daughter. The old lady was all shriveled up, and her daughter was pretty old, too. She was a chain smoker, had large yellow teeth, and read romance novels constantly. When her pet canary died, she carried it in her apron pocket for days and took it out from time to time to look at it, pet it, and talk to it.

One day, I was in our garden trying out an infantry trenching tool that I'd found, when I heard some shots from the direction of the house. Grandfather was a few feet from the door with his hands up in the air, and a Russian soldier facing him, pointing his machine gun at him. My brother, Alex, was standing close to grandfather.

Afterward, we figured that the soldier demanded wine. Grandfather could speak some Serbian, which is close to Russian.

When grandfather said we didn't have any wine, the soldier fired some rounds over his head. When that didn't work either, he fired some rounds across Grandfather's chest.

The old man went down hard and lay on his back. Alex ran. Mother and Grandmother were coming out to see what the shots were about and fell on Grandfather, screaming. When they pulled his shirt apart, we could see several small red holes across his chest. Grandfather tried to say something, at least his mouth was moving. He didn't manage to get any words out. His mouth was filling up with blood. The screaming annoyed the soldier. He waived with his gun for them to go back in the house. Mother was in hysterics and didn't respond. We pulled her off Grandfather and dragged her into the house. The soldier then turned and walked off. He seemed very young.

We didn't know what to do with Grandfather. The next day a Russian officer told us to bury him. We rolled him in a tar paper and buried him in the yard by the far fence. One of the Russian soldiers helped dig the hole and helped us pull Grandfather into it.

A few days later, Alex made a wooden cross and was burning Grandfather's name on it with a magnifying glass, when a group of soldiers noticed what he was doing and seemed impressed by the magnifying glass. One asked if Alex could light his cigarette with it. When he did, the soldier tried to tell him he wanted it and started to take some money from his pocket. Another soldier just reached over, grabbed it from Alex, and walked off with it.

Over 30 years ago many feared the atomic bomb would bring an end to civilization. Tom Lehrer, a noted satirist came up with these lines as part of a song, "We'll all burn together when we burn. We'll all go together when we go."

We Are All in it Together
Luther Mandell
(d. Jan. 2003)

Think back, we've been on a memory trail for a time, and while certain incidents stand out, the years become a blur.

We were children at six playing games, we were know-it-alls at sixteen, trying to find our way to the future. At twenty six we were proud of our progeny. At 56 and 76 we are using our strong minds in conjunction with strong bodies, to pass on to the future that which we have encountered and witnessed in the past.

I challenge you to look not only to the past, but also the future. To be stuck in the past is a sure route to oblivion. You have nothing to offer but memories. Think back. Most of us were born between the two World Wars. Think of the conditions, social as well of financial that existed then, in contrast to today, racial relations, sexual issues, the aid to the elderly, the handicapped, the poor. Those changes didn't just happen. We made those happen, nor are we through. We never will be.

But as long as we look to the future and say to ourselves, "This must change and be fixed" and use our voices and efforts to make it happen, it will happen. Slowly, yes, but inevitably. What we do for ourselves will aid those who follow. As night follows day, as youth becomes aged, our needs become their needs. Therefore, it is essential that as we see the light, and are recruited to the cause, we make life more viable, physically, socially, and financially.

Today we have easier access to buildings for the handicapped, ease at the curb for anyone infirm. Modern medicine keeps many of us alive. Educational opportunities, classes like writing, computers, and fitness keep our brains active and bring seniors out of their homes and into a more vibrant life. Life does not stop at 65 or 75. It goes on as long as our brains function.

Our excursions "down memory lane" are invaluable. They help us look into the future. It keeps us all in it together.

Those who work in the eye of the storm do not pause to consider cause and effect. Their sole purpose is to do what needs to be done in the moment, and to do it well. Thus, it is often difficult to give an answer to a direct question of how and what.

Preparing The Way

Dawn McFarland

On the way home from a Hospice meeting last night my friend asked what it was that a Chaplain *did* for people. The tenor of his voice was almost a challenge and I felt like I was standing behind home plate when someone suddenly threw a ball from outfield and I was unprepared to catch it.

Defensively, I wondered what I could say to give him not only an understanding, but an assurance that even with pastors and volunteers the work of a chaplain was a vital one.

As I cogitated over this I let my thoughts travel backwards to my own time as a hospital chaplain. First on the oncology ward, then in the trauma room. Both of these were intense settings and the daily dramas enacted there could cause burnout if one did not debrief afterward. I will not soon forget the first confrontation I had with death - as a chaplain.

It was the weekend of my first week in Pastoral Care as an intern. I had dropped by the department only to pick up a booklet when one of the Senior Chaplains asked me to ride up in the elevator with him. He was on his way to support the parents of a chronologically twenty year old girl with the mind of a three year old. She had been in and out of the hospital many times and since she was now only an artificially supported breathing vegetable the time had come to turn off the machines. He had spent considerable time with them during -previous hospitalizations.. Before I really knew what was happening, Ellis' floor came up and he took my arm and escorted me down the hall. What? He expected me to go with him? Three days into my training? I had had no floor experience as yet - surely not me? It is just now, as

I type these words, that I realize why he did that.

No, it was not to be likened to throwing a child into shallow water to teach him to swim. It was more like knowing you had a life buoy to hang onto before you took the plunge. He asked me because he would need me. When the dastardly deed was done - when he had witnessed life being deliberately snuffed out, he would need someone to turn to - someone who had "been there-done that" and he knew I had. Wow!

He spoke to the charge nurse, was briefed on current status of events and entered the room quietly with me closely behind. The parents appeared close to the senior years. It may be that all the trials of having a child who was "different" had worn them down and prematurely aged them, but they looked as though they had never been young. Sitting on either side of the bed, they each held their daughter's hand. The young woman in the bed looked like a gigantic blown up doll. Round impish face, pixie curls but her blue eyes stared vacantly at the ceiling. The father reached to the bed stand and picked up a tiny cassette player, on it he placed one of her favorite tunes. Then he put it close to her ear, speaking very softly, he explained what he was doing and it seemed a smile brightened her face for a moment, but I wondered if I had imagined it. The music played on and on. We made some conversation, but it was forced. Ellis asked if they would like him to read something and they chose a favorite psalm. A male nurse was in and out several times as Ellis read. Then we all repeated the Lord's Prayer in unison. Then a nod from the father brought the nurse quickly to the bed where he turned off the machines.

The startling stillness shook us from our silent reveries as the music slowly faded as though it were an affront to continue where consenting conspirators had fought with death and finally yielded.

The quiet became deafening. The Chaplain moved to the father so I reached out to the mother. Not a word was spoken but there was strong support in the arms that enveloped them and we could readily ascertain their appreciation as they briefly leaned on us and gathered strength. Several moments had passed when the nurse appeared with a certificate to sign and the question that nurses, chaplains, doctors hate to ask.

But it must be asked quickly. "Do you want to donate any organs for medical use."

As many times and as many different ways as I have used to approach this question it never comes easily. If I knew the family ahead of time, it was sometimes easier to prepare the way so that at the final moment it need not be discussed again. In this case, the parents were affronted at such a question. Medicine and doctors had done enough, they said, don't violate her more.

The director of the institution where the girl had lived asked the nurse if he could speak to the parents and they went out to meet with him. Ellis and I went out also to attend to the necessary paperwork expected of our department. But once outside the door, my senior worker turned to me and held out his arms. We held each other up, literally, for the strain had been so great that it would have been all too easy to sink to the floor and rest, saying "It is finished." He thanked me and we went our separate ways.

The readying of family for such a procedure, staying with them, handling business arrangements as much as possible, all this is the role of a chaplain.

I was startled from my reverie by my companion repeating his question.

"Fred, I said, "Let me tell you a story."

Storm on The Moon

Ariel Edmundson

There's a storm on the moon,
Black clouds scurrying past.
Leaving no light in the room.
Night is covered with a dark mask,
Strange restless moods swirl and spin,
A tree branch bends and snaps in the wind.

This story recalls a simple Japanese-American farm family displaced by the Second World War. Sent to a camp in the desert at Manzanar. They lost their simple way of life, I lost a friend.

The Day I Ate Orange Guck

Roger E. Honzik

I don't know just how old I was when I became really aware of that funny little man who lived by the sea. Perhaps I had seen him when I was three or four but one thing I know; when I was five I talked to him. That was a few years before the beginning of the Second World War.

Our family had a special fishing place at the ocean a little past the old lighthouse at Palos Verde's in Southern California. The lighthouse was built on a large rocky point of land just north of Long Beach Harbor; it was a perfect fishing area.

The little old man I mentioned was a farmer who lived with his family on the high palisades overlooking the Pacific Ocean. These humble people planted lima beans and chickpeas on that narrow strip of land above the rocky shores of our fishing spot. Just crude hand tools and a determination born of years of struggle gave them a simple kind of life.

As we would cross their fields on the way to the edge of the cliff, dad would honk the old Chevy horn and I would wave. The old man would look but I never recall that he returned my wave, yet somehow he was my friend. He would look and then bend back down to work; we would hike down to the ocean and catch our fish.

Sometimes his family was down at the ocean too. I would carefully watch them as I fished, for they were a strange and different people. It might have been the first time I saw them by the water that I spoke to the old man. I don't remember what I said but I do know he said, "toot-toot" and then he smiled and went on wading among the rocks and seaweed.

Later he climbed out onto a large rock and he emptied a small sack he had filled with abalone. Bait I thought, but so much and they don't even have fishing poles. What happened next was unbelievable to me. He sat on a large rough rock and took a medium size abalone and broke the shell away from the meat. He then rubbed the meat against the rough stone. That seemed to sand off the black and also took off some of the tough edges of the abalone. Next he washed it, and ate the whole thing bite by bite as though it were an apple.

On later visits to the coast, my old friend gave me some raw abalone to taste. Another time some kelp, I called sea lettuce, and once he gave me some small black mussels to try. I would talk to him, but he would only smile in return.

The last day I remember seeing the old man, it was blustery and cold, a very wintry day. He waded out of the water and showed me a bag of bright purple sea urchins he had just gathered. He sat down near me and rubbed one gently on a rock to remove some of the sharp spines. He gently turned the urchin upside down, and with a small rock, he carefully cracked off the bottom third of the globe like shell. There they were, two sacks of bright orange roe amid some lesser sticky looking things. With a small pair of sticks he offered one sack to me. My mind swam perhaps my stomach too, as I took that orange guck with my fingers. Did I eat it? Yes, because you must always trust a friend. The taste had a rich salty tang like the smell of the sea. Even today they taste, well, very special to me. As I savor that flavor I think of my friend of so long ago.

We never saw the little old man or his family after that day. I later was told that his kind was
rounded up and sent to a camp on the high desert, a place called Manzanar.

I was told to hate so young.

War can make a boy into a man; but at what cost?

Glenn Comes Home

Barbara Lang

I'm guessing that in every large family, there is one rebel son. In ours, it was my brother, Glenn. Glenn seemed to always be in trouble; he was a relentless tease, and I did get mad at him, but I seldom told on him. Who could stay mad at such a charmer? My brother was two years older than I; we were buddies, co-conspirators, sharing everything from marbles to bicycles.

We made soapbox cars out of orange crates and old skate wheels to sail down the hill. We built forts in the empty lot across the street. Glenn was even able to bribe me into playing cops and robbers or cowboys and Indians.

Our sister, Joanne, was just fifteen months older than Glenn. He was the bane of her life. She didn't think he was funny, and was mortified to have to be in the same schoolroom, where he persisted in being the class entertainer, making wisecracks, shooting spitballs, or tripping someone in the aisles. Notes went home from teachers, saying: "Glenn is a bright boy, and could do better if he applied himself." At home, he delighted in playing practical jokes on Jo.

Even as a young kid, Glenn was a born salesman, instinctively knowing how to pour on the charm to get results. The guy could sell anything. Mom, always looking for ways to supplement the family income, made doughnuts and popcorn balls for Glenn to sell at summer softball games in the park. Glenn always had at least one paper route. And if he could gather enough neighborhood suckers, he formed marble games, playing for keeps or for pennies. Mom said that Glenn was the reason for her prematurely grey hair.

Glenn and I went to boarding school the same year, he a junior, and I a freshman. He lasted almost one semester, before the Dean of boys and the Principal decided it would be best if he would "voluntarily withdraw." The reasons given to his parents were: Insubordination, and an inability to fit into the program.

After finishing high school at home, Glenn decided to follow in the footsteps of his older brother, Les, and joined the Marine Corp. Mom didn't want to sign for him, he was only seventeen. But I think Dad thought it was probably a good idea.

During the long, dreary winter months of 1950-1951, our family feared that the worse had happened. Glenn had been sent to Korea immediately after completing boot camp and special training in communications. America was deeply involved in what was then called the "Korean Conflict." Glenn was in the First Division, 5th Regiment, trained to be a lineman, and was with the first units to land in Inchon to install communication lines. We had not heard from him for months. The only news we had was what we read in the newspapers, or heard from Drew Pearson on the radio, and that wasn't good.

We knew that the winter was bitter cold in Korea and the leathernecks were not equipped for the freezing weather. We heard that soldiers lacked warm clothing and were suffering frost bite. Feeling helpless, and needing to keep busy, our mother faithfully packed and mailed boxes of warm socks, gloves, homemade cookies, candy and magazines to her son, not knowing if he was missing in action or worse. We learned later he never received any of the care packages.

Finally, with the assistance of the Red Cross, we learned that Glenn was in a hospital in Tokyo, recuperating from a foot injury; his jeep had overturned after hitting a land mine near the Choisin Reservoir. The injury had not been serious, but his stay in the hospital was prolonged when he contracted Hepatitis. He had been one sick marine, and assumed that we had been notified. Later, he told us the story of the first Marine withdrawal in history.

Until about mid November of 1950, the Marines had never fought anyway but forward. Their stories of Guadacanal and Iwo Jima were legend, where many thousands had died but never had they ceased a battle until "the objective was secure." That was the history of the Marines. But in November of 1950, the 5th Marines fought an exhausting five day and five night battle out of the freezing communist trap on the west side of the Changjin Reservoir. It had been worse than anything in Marine history; the men were exhausted, had faced death and somehow survived. Although the Colonel emphatically insisted

"This is no retreat. This is an assault in another direction," the men took the withdrawal hard.

Glenn, along with his unit, began the terrible trek out of the purple and white mountains of Northeastern Korea, which cost nearly

5000 dead, wounded or frostbitten marines. A hard price for America to pay, for once again underestimating the Soviet-sponsored Chinese.

The bloody trail out of "Nightmare Alley" showed that even a marine supported by air and the best weapons of the time, could not fend of masses of howling Chinese soldiers when they outnumbered him twenty or thirty to one. Later, Lt. Col. John Stevens, commander of the first battalion, 5th Marines said, "What we needed, was more men. We found out that you can't fight a halfhearted war; we have to go all out, or get out."

The 1st Marine Division had begun pushing north from Hamhung on the narrow, winding road leading to the Changjin Reservoir. The fifth Marines were ordered to cross snowy mountain passes to seize the town of Yudam-ni. There were reports of a Chinese buildup just outside the town, born out by heavy attacks on their supply lines. Soon a massive Chinese offensive slashed at the 8th Army, driving them back many miles and stripping the marines of protection. There was no doubt that great hordes of Chinese must be swarming over the mountain ridges separating the two American forces.

Even so, the marines were ordered to keep advancing. Then the worst happened. Between six and eight Chinese divisions, estimates ranged from 80,000 to 120,000 men—struck at the marines, now strung out from Changjin Reservoir back to Koto. The 5th and 7th Regiments were trapped at Yudam-ni. The steep-sided valleys led to Yudam-ni along a narrow, ice-glazed road , providing the Chinese with clear targets. The Marines fought hard, but the next day, orders came to fight their way back from Yudam-ni to Hagaru.

Guns and vehicles froze. The marines had to chip ice off the mortars to fire them. The wounded had no choice but to take their chances in the convoy under attack. Whole platoons were slaughtered.

On December third, the ten-mile long caravan finally reached Hagaru plateau. The marines were still acting as a unit. They had cracked roadblocks, fixed bridges under fire and suffered anguish, when, time after time, Chinese swooped into their midst flinging hand grenades into truckloads of screaming wounded. Glenn was one of the 4500 wounded and frostbite cases flown out of Hagaru strip.

Only those men who absolutely must be flown out, would go.

Every man who could shoot was needed for fighting through a solid Chinese wall. The men were exhausted, faces swollen from the cold and bleeding from the icy wind, many of them hatless by now, their ears blue in the frost. Some walked to the doctor's tent barefooted, unable to get their frostbitten feet into their frozen boots.

On December 8th, Glenn had his nineteenth Birthday in the Tokoyo Hospital. He had recovered from his injury, and his request to return to his unit was granted, in spite of some lingering effects of Hepatitis. Finally, in he spring of 1951, we received word that he was coming home; his ship would dock in the San Francisco Bay.

Because we weren't sure which ship, or which day, we listened to the news on the radio and checked the newspapers. Dad, who would rather take a beating than drive in San Francisco, willingly made several trips to the docks, each time scanning the ship, the decks crowded with thousands of waving, cheering servicemen. Twice, Mom and Dad would drive home, disappointed. The third time, Glenn's ship was there, with thousands of other military personnel. How lucky we were! He would be home on leave for a few weeks before returning to Camp Pendleton.

The first few days after the homecoming were a blur of excitement, stories to be told, news to catch up on, home cooking to eat, and dates with Nancy, who had waited for him. I found myself studying my brother. The curly-headed, fun loving, prankster who left home a year and a half ago, was now a stranger to me. Glenn didn't want to talk much about Korea, and the buddies he lost there. There was a restlessness about him; he had trouble concentrating. He had taken up chain smoking. Sometimes in the night, Joanne, whose bedroom was next to his, heard him shout out in his nightmares. He was fighting the Gooks on Nightmare Alley.

With the routine of daily living and passing of time, life for our family took on some of the old familiar normalcy. But nothing would ever be quite the same for the young Marine who had put on a uniform and sailed to hell and back. That sensitive, screw-up kid had been left somewhere back on the road to Hagaru.

Just reminiscing about the not so good old days in Berettyoujfalu, Hungary.

Coming of Age

Laszlo Daroczi

At first it was Charlie, then Alex, who dumped me. We used to roam the country-side and I was glad to tag along. From time to time those two would argue over which one I would go with when they had different places in mind. I enjoyed that status. Now, I was ignored because they started to like girls.

Alex was in the school folk dance group and they would go to neighboring towns on some weekends. I was lost. How could they like girls? Girls ran funny and giggled a lot. They didn't seem interesting at all. Alex would tie a kerchief on his head overnight to press a wave in his hair. He and Charlie were now meticulous in keeping clean and presentable. It was a good thing I had my reading to fall back on. Joe, for some reason, hardly ever came along with us, even in the best of times. He had his friends and went his separate way.

Father bought a lot to grow vegetables across town. On weekends in good weather he'd go there to cultivate it. He took me along more than the other boys to work there. I had to push the wheelbarrow with the garden tools. I sure didn't want to be seen by my classmates, rattling along on the macadam stone road, especially the girls.

By now, Grandfather had died of cancer. When I looked in the window, he was lying on the bed. His face looked yellow. Wailing women were raising a lot of hue and cry. They followed the funeral procession out to the cemetery. I sure didn't miss him at all. I don't think anybody else did, either. Father may have, but you never knew how he felt about things. He wasn't into displays of affection. He and mother fought a lot. He tried to out-shout her and she, of course, was no doormat.

When Alex was arrested and sent away, life became harder again. Alex had organized a group of boys, mostly classmates, to oppose the system. They would meet as a pseudo-study group in a basement room in school. I was too young to be a full-fledged member, but I did go to most meetings. The group stole a radio from another school to listen to The Voice of America and Radio Free Europe. We didn't pick up much, because these broadcasts were jammed. After a while, they decided to return the radio. They smashed it, and returned it in a basket with a note saying, "This is how we will smash you, Communists."

Alex also typed up some anti-communist slogans, which we pasted on fences around town. The paste we made from flour and water. The way Alex got caught was when they botched an attempt to blow up the Russian Memorial in the middle of town with a hand grenade. It was to blow up the eve of a holiday commemorating the liberation of the country by the glorious red army.

They drew lots as to who would actually put the explosive there and light the fuse. The fuse was home made. It was thick yarn soaked in kerosene. By the time the boy waited for the foot traffic to die and laid out the yarn, it just did not want to stay lit. It was a windy night, and some of the kerosene must have evaporated, too. He finally got cold feet and ran home. But he left the explosive at the base of the Memorial, and that's where it was found after the honor guard was posted a few feet from it.

The next morning, they searched high and low until they searched the school. There they found a few more explosives in the study room used by the underground group. They were hidden in the unused tile stove. The Russians rounded all of the boys up in a few days. When they learned that I had attended the meetings, as well, two men in civilian clothes came in a car to take me in for questioning. It was the first time I was in a passenger vehicle.

The only thing they kept asking was whether father listened to the Voice of America and Free Europe broadcasts. They were nice enough, but I was terrified. No, father knew nothing about any of this, which of course was true. When they got to their headquarters, they didn't want to question me anymore, and told me to go home. I was happy to do that.

Alex and the others were not tortured. Alex said later, they stood him facing a wall for hours on end, then questioned him again and again. He was finally tried and sentenced to six years of forced labor. Father was tried as well and was sentenced to one year of concentration camp, even though he knew absolutely nothing about any of this. His health was ruined during his sentence. He had a bad case of stomach ulcers. When they took father away, there was no income for the family. Charlie, the oldest brother, dropped out of school and became the bread-winner.

In school I was taller than most of my classmates and also skinnier than most. Being tall, I was fairly high in the pecking order. One day I got into a fight with a classmate and got kicked out of school. Actually, I never hit the other kid, but the teacher who looked out on the school yard saw me on top of the kid and that was enough. The kid was about my size but quite pudgy. Certainly, no fighter. For that matter, I was not one either.

It happened fast. After shouting back and forth for a minute, the other kids formed a circle around us and were eager to see a fight, I think. We were both surprised, because neither of us intended to fight. But once the ring was formed, we squared off. I stepped toward him and he stepped back and tripped and fell right on his back. I, of course, pounced on him and the fight was over without either of us even swinging at the other.

In a couple of days I was transferred to the other elementary school in town. I didn't know any of the kids there. When they found out I was kicked out of school for fighting, they regarded me with awe. I was automatically on top of the pecking order.

The seventh and eighth grades I finished in one year in an accelerated program because of the year lost during the war. This was a coed class and I showed off consistently in front of the girls. Now I began to understand why Charlie, then Alex, dropped me like a hot potato when they started liking girls. I started to carry a comb.

My first love note was an agonizing experience. I tossed it over at Miriam and it landed on the seat next to her. She didn't see it. I was sitting on pins and needles.

What would I say to her after she read the note? When the bell sounded for recess, she stood up and walked out. I ran over and picked up the note. I never tried again and never got any closer to Miriam. When the occasion came now and then to talk with her, I became completely tongue-tied. She had no idea what a huge crush I had on her. When she started to go with a kid who was in a class ahead of us, I plotted to beat him to a pulp. I was bigger. When I saw them together, they talked and talked. When she went to the swimming pool with her parents, he would join them and even talked intelligently with her parents.

Girls, all of them, seemed to live in a parallel universe which was totally alien to me.

V. Sideshow Wonders

Voices of Variety

At the risk of sounding sacrilegious, I have written this story comparing an estate sale to church. It should "go to show you" that religion is where you find it.

Sunday Morning

Dick Cory

It is 8:30a.m. this Sunday morning and the congregation is waiting outside the church of the Estate Yard Sale. The deacons and deaconesses are busily organizing the communion tables full of treasures from the departed soul. A flaxen rope separates the anxious parishioners from entering this hallowed ground until the service begins. Only Saint John's Catholic Church will have more in attendance this early spring day. All of God's children seem to be "up" for this anticipated event.

The rope drops precisely as the hour hand reaches nine. Hordes of brethren nearly trample one another as they scurry to the pearly gates of the "churches'" entrance. There is barely room as these religious fervents squeeze through the doorway. Fortunately, once inside, the crowd spreads out to the treasure laden tables in the various rooms. There one finds beads, chalices, paintings, robes and altars of furniture. Most of the items can be purchased for less than a tithe.

The commandment of thou shalt not covet is soon forgotten as the collectors scramble for these holy treasures. Still the throng, which now seems made up of heathens, continues to be entering this sacred domain. Some arrive with empty baskets with which to gather gifts of glory; others bring vessels containing water or coffee with which to anoint one another.

The feeding frenzy continues for more than two hours in this shopper's synagogue. The people leverage past one another, arms loaded and elbows extended to protect their scavenged treasures. I move like an amoeba being squeezed partly by the crowd, but generally in the direction I wish to go. Finally, I arrive at the room that I've been seeking; the study sanctuary. Books lining the shelves are organized by section and each one is priced. By the time I get there, all of the free ones are taken. The gentleman in front of me blocks my view of the travel and history section. I move to the left. He moves to the left. I move to the right. He moves to the right. A lady slithers in front of both of us heading to another section. I remind myself that patience is a virtue and of the commandment " thou shalt not kill". Eventually the man in front of me moves on and I get seconds.

Trying to read titles through my bifocals while trying to see the broader picture requires that I remove and then replace my glasses on my nose. It's more frustrating than studying scripture from a small print bible. Finally I become less selective and gather any that remotely resemble my interest.

The line at the moneychanger's table has already formed when I start my exodus towards the door. Not being willing to relinquish my booty and now trapped in the slowly moving procession, my arms ache to relinquish the burden of the load. I practice ZEN "medication". We move forward with the speed of an entourage of rosary fondling, chanting monks.

By the time I reach the treasurer, my hands are so numb that I can hardly get change from my pocket. Greed has led me down this lane like a sacrificial lamb.

Trade is so active that the money collector forgets that the stack of bills next to her on the table should have been placed in the collection box. She asks, "Is this your money?" I say, "No," and remember the commandment, "Thou shalt not steal." My offering is made and I move toward the door. Surely goodness and mercy will follow me as I make my recession from this holy church of the Estate Sale.

Hey to That City by The Bay

Ariel Edmundson

Hey to that City by the bay
To the Marina, the Sunset, the Richmond
The Mission and the Western Addition
To Haight and Love
That city by the Bay,
Bury your hash
Don't cover the City with trash.
Walk in Golden Gate Park
Never after dark.
Hey to the City by the Bay
Pigeons sick in the square
Please don't feed them there
Homeless on the street
Begging quarters for something to eat
Hey to the City by the Bay
When Earth Quake III Splits it in two
All will vanish into the sea
We'll not live to see the next century
Hey to that City by the Bay
It will be missed some fine day
Foghorns on the Bay moan its fate
No one is left to appreciate
Sunsets on the Golden Gate

Elizabeth Garrett composed the New Mexico state song, officially adopted in 1917. I first met her when I was a young girl going to high school in Roswell, New Mexico. She is a lady that I shall never forget.

Miss Garrett

Florence Johanson

  The dog starts barking as soon as I put one foot on the long walkway that leads from the sidewalk to the small cottage at the back of the property. I hesitate. I am afraid of barking dogs and this one sounds big and fierce! Gingerly, I take another step hoping the dog is barking at someone else. It isn't. It's me, all right, but I keep resolutely moving forward. I have to go. I am expected! The dog's bark grows louder and I use all my will power. I want to turn tail and run in the opposite direction. I am afraid of dogs, but I am afraid of a lot of other things as well---things like meeting new people and going alone to places I have never been before.
  As my trembling fingers press the doorbell, the bark is approaching a double fortissimo and I have lost control of my knees! The door opens and, suddenly, I am face to face with an immense German Shepherd and Miss Garrett is greeting me warmly and pulling me forward while trying to calm the dog. Tina and I are introduced but I can tell that we are not destined to become close friends. In fact, I want to stay as far away from Tina as possible and I endeavor to keep Miss Garrett between us as we move to the grand piano. Miss Garrett explains that Tina is very protective. I am amazed and relieved when, at a sharp command from her mistress, she settles quietly at what I guess to be her usual post by the window and Miss Garrett begins my first voice lesson.
  This is a big day in my life. I love to sing and have always wanted to take lessons.
  Miss Garrett is famous in New Mexico. A graduate of the prestigious Julliard School of Music, she is the composer of our official

New Mexico state song. She explains to me that, if I do well with my lessons, and wish to continue with music, she can get me into Julliard. I am thrilled!

When a soft ringing sounds from the watch around Miss Garrett's neck, she opens the front of the case and carefully touches the hands. The lesson time is over.

In the tiny kitchen, I watch as Miss Garrett pours water into a singing kettle and makes tea for us. I watch in awe of this amazing feat because, you see, Miss Garrett is blind. She has been since birth!

Many years have passed since my first encounter with that remarkable woman and I was to learn much more than music from her. Most of all, she taught me of the indomitability of the human spirit. That it is possible to rise above great handicap, even blindness.

Miss Garrett, who was the daughter of the famous Pat Garrett of Billy the Kid fame, lived alone in her own home. Her seeing-eye dog, Tina, was given to her by the state of New Mexico in appreciation for the state song. She was a woman who saw beauty in the sounds and scents around her, in the things she touched, in the song of the bird and ripple of the water; in the warmth of sunshine on her face and the fragrance of roses. The simple songs she composed in her lifetime told of her joy and love for these things. She was proud of her Mexican heritage and she made sure that I learned to sing some of our folk songs in the Spanish language. She said that some day, when I no longer lived in New Mexico, I would cherish those songs, as they were part of MY heritage.

I think she lived in the little house until the end of her life, which came suddenly. Tina died and a year later Miss Garrett slipped on the steps of the Methodist Church. She had never adjusted to the new seeing-eye dog.

When I heard of Miss Garrett's death, I realized that I would never forget the lessons she taught and the way she enriched my young life.

Magic Night

Ariel Edmundson

Magic night transposes
In moonlight grow silver roses.
Night blooming jasmine holds its breath
As summer day goes to rest.
A cricket concert magically begins
As the sun floats below the ocean brim.
Golden dreams come true at night
And vanish in morning light.

This story relates a fun experience I shared with my mother-in-law. Were she still living, we would enjoy a laugh and the education we got for a buck.

All You Can Carry For a Buck

Dick Cory

That's what the sign at the top of the stairs says. My mother-in-law, Frances, spotted this one-day sale ad in the Lincoln Journal and Star. Both of us, being packrat teachers, cannot resist this tempting challenge. We only have twenty minutes to complete the "heist" as my wife, Feona, is sitting in the illegally parked get-away car, our 1968 gutless Plymouth Fury II.

This is Nebraska School Book Depository with discards from around the state. How can school boards let these pearls of wisdom and learning slip through their hands? Soon we are harvesting, rescuing these study "waifs" from the burn pile (it is 1971 and recycling is not yet on the scene).

Some would look at us as patriots, recycling education from the rich districts to the poor. My mother-in-law is a gracious large woman who embraces a book with the same loving care that she has for her sandhills pupils. Her one room schoolhouse never has enough learning materials but this is no fault of hers. Her accomplice, me, is a scavenging science teacher from California. This adventure is but one more learning event for the two of us who are attending summer school classes at Nebraska Wesleyan.

Hurriedly we search the piles strewn on the floor of this upstairs warehouse. Time is fleeting and the challenge of "all that you can carry" is ever present. Soon our time elapses and we trudge, struggling to carry our loot, to the checkout table. We make fun of each other as we compare piles and pay our dollars.

Still the problem of negotiating the twenty-two steps to the ground floor, books in hand, remains. The stairway is narrow with no handrails. Was this a gag being played on us by Candid Camera?

I let my mother-in-law go first. As I tell her, if we fall at least I'll have something soft to land on. She chuckles and waddles with her outstretched armload of books as she descends the stairway.

Her elbows rub against the sidewalls as she carefully takes each step. She's only able to feel each level with her foot as the books obscure her vision. My trip down is equally difficult, but I refuse to let Frances show me up.

Miraculously, we make it to the sidewalk below. We throw the armloads of books into the get-away car, pile into the seats, and leave in a Fury. I check the rearview mirror, but no cops are in sight. Our caper goes without a hitch.

Upon our return to the singlewide trailer that we have rented for the summer, we unload and compare our bounties. We debate as to who has got the most books for their buck. Frances claims victory as she says her seventeen beats my sixteen pieces. I refuse to accept her claim, telling her that the mass of my books exceeds hers. I should win. She agrees to acquiesce if I can offer proof.

Since we have no scale, we devise a balance using a rope to suspend a broomstick from the clothesline crossbar. The stick is carefully balanced with no load in place. Then we hang a ten-pound sack of potatoes as a counter balance from one side of the broomstick, and a shopping bag of books from the other side. This works fine as we measure the mass of books in units of potatoes. My books have a greater mass of three potatoes. This proves that I have carried the more massive load. It was a moot point as we both claim victory and a wonderful day. Those unsuspecting folks back at the book depository will never know what entertainment they provide.

The following is a bit of fantasy after a true personal experience. Standing on the huge Wintergarden stage in New York City, looking out to the emptyness where an unembodied voice told me to begin, then said "Thank you, that will be all", was never to be forgotten. I fantasize.

Audition At The Wintergarden

Alison K. Paolini

Alone, but one of many,
She stood small in a large space.
From the darkness past the proscenium
Came a voice asking her name.
A strong voice, but in a hurry and not friendly.
She looked around.
In the harsh lighting she felt pale,
In the harsh lighting she sought warmth.

Off in the wings others were waiting,
Much as she had waited.
Off in the wings people were going on
About their business.
The floor boards were bare.
The floor boards were worn.
The floor boards had stories to tell.

Time stopped.
She thought she heard Ethel Merman,
No, Mary Martin ... or Barbra Steisand.
That could have been Liza Minelli!
But this is now and that was then.

Flash! She was still alone in a large space.
Above hung ropes and beams.
Above were catwalks and ladders.

Lighting fixtures filled the space.
Curtains suspended in rows,

Creating the only warmth by their
Velvet sheen of deep wine.

Time stopped once more.
A breeze lifted the hair off her neck.
She sensed movement,
Possibly a ballet.
Certainly she felt vibrations.

A voice broke in ...
Did she have music, what was it?
Did she have music, what key?
Did she have music?
She peered into the darkness,
And answered.
Her music passed to the pianist.
She told him her key.
With one false start, she sang.

True clear tones.
Fresh interpretation!
A transformation ...
She grew in stature ... filling the stage..
She drew all eyes and ears.
No longer seeming to be a small girl in a large space,
She created an image.
She created a moment.
She shared a sound, and aura.
In years to come her voice would be
Remembered ..
Here at the
Wintergarden Theatre.

When Betsy, our first dog died, I vowed not to have another dog again, but Gary, my husband, decided otherwise. I am glad he did, because now I cannot imagine life without Kelly.

Kelly

Norma Obitz

I was lying on the day bed watching Mommy write about Betsy. I cannot understand why she still thinks of her. She's been gone for more than 3 years now. Why doesn't she just write about me? While she was pondering about Betsy, I also started strolling down memory lane.

I was just a newborn when my real mom left me in the pound. I didn't like that place so I knew I had to do something about it. To survive, I knew I had to be cunning, so when the administrator of the pound was about to describe me on the form, I gave him a nudge, and tried to look as cute as I could, then I curled up to appear as small as possible. It worked; he described me as Toy Fox Terrier. It was not long before I went home with my first mommy. The adoption didn't work out and it was for the best ,as she was mean, hitting me whenever I did something. I had just been born so I did not know how to behave. She should have taught me, but she was working and did not have the time. As soon as she arrived home, I would just cower, thinking she was about to hit me. When she was told that I would be a big dog, she took me back to the pound. In a way, I was glad; maybe I could find someone who would love and treat me better. God, whoever you are, please make it soon, because pretty soon no one will want me. I am growing every day you know.

One morning in March, I woke up and had this feeling that this would be the day I would be chosen. That feeling was crushed when they put four puppies in with me. They were cute and very small. Prospective parents prefer small dogs, so my chance of being chosen that day was slim to none. I just had to use my wits so people would notice me more; but every time I looked at my four new roommates, my hopes were dashed. God, do you hear me? Can you just make these puppies uglier, or just make them invisible, just for today? I know I will be chosen if not for them, please, please.

A car pulled onto the parking lot, and I could see everything from my cage. The couple seemed to be serious about getting a dog, and not just looky-lous. I heard a voice saying that these were my new parents, so I prepared myself to impress them. Just my luck, the woman was oriental. Word is, they are not fond of dogs; she could be more of a Cruela than my first mom. But I have to get out of here before they give me the needle.

They came in, and the man noticed me, pointing at me. I quickly put my left ear up; every one thinks I look cute with one ear up, and it also makes me look smarter, I think. It is so pathetic, as that is the only trick I know. If only my first mommy taught me some tricks. Oh please, please let him pick me. I should block these other mutts. I am bigger, I could do it. If they see them, they surely will pick one of them.

Oh no, I am not big enough to block them, oh please, please, don't let them see these puppies. They are now staring at us, I will do the sad and pitiful face, then fold my ears on top of my head; we'll see if they can resist that.

"We should look in Chico," I heard her saying to him. I was right. She is another Cruela, and now they're leaving. Well, I guess the voice in my head this morning was wrong, but tomorrow is another day and I should not lose hope. I do not know how long I still have before you know what. My time is running out, I must find a home soon.

This has turned out to be a sad day, I was sure when I saw them that they would be my new parents, how could I be wrong. It was almost closing time when I heard a car pulling into the parking lot. It's them, they have come back for me.

Please, God, don't let me be wrong. Suddenly I was led out of the cage. "You can play with her to see if you will like her," said the guard. I should behave and not scare them; I should kiss up to the guy, as the woman seems to be very hard to impress.

We sat on the bench and he let me loose. I just sat in front of him, putting my ears up, turning my head side to side, trying to look as cute as I could and on my very best behavior. It's working, he's petting me, it is a good sign.

"What do you think?" he asked.

"Her paws are kind of large, she could grow to be a large dog.

"I really don't like big dogs," she replied.
"It says she is a Toy fox Terrier."
"It is up to you," she finally said.
"Okay, we'll take her."
Oh, thank you God, whoever you are, I am finally out of here.

On our way home, I heard her say, "As soon as we get to the house, carry her directly to the tub and bathe her; she stinks." I wanted to tell her, "If you lived in that cage, you would stink too." I guess a bath is not bad. I just hope they will not make a habit of bathing me, I hate water. We finally got home and after the bath, she toweled me dry and brushed my fur. She is not so bad after all, I think I am going to like her, too. I am content now with a mommy and a daddy. I will try my best to behave so they will not return me to that awful place.

Every morning we take a walk but dad gets tired because I drag him so they decided to enroll me in this obedience class. I hate the class, too many dogs, some are cute, some are uglier than me, most are bigger and the small ones are show offs. The class did not last because there was no improvement in my behavior, so they gave up.

I am no longer afraid of being taken back to the pound because I know they would never do that to me. Why am I so sure of myself, you ask? Well, one day they went to Walgreens and left me in the car. I thought they had abandoned me. I started to panic, and as a consequence, lost control and pooped on the seat. Even I could not stand the smell. I was really afraid, remembering my first mom and how she hit me every time I did a bad thing, and this was major bad thing. As expected, when they opened the door, Mommy was particularly furious, as I did it on her seat. If looks could kill, I would be dead by now.

I thought she would hit me, so, I cowered, waiting for it, but it did not happen. She just yelled, "bad dog, bad dog!" while they cleaned up the mess. On the way home, Mommy was still furious. She was talking nonstop about me.

"I can't believe you talked me into getting this dog, she is not at all like Betsy. First, she is retarded, did not learn anything in the obedience class. Second, she grows every day. Toy Fox Terrier, my foot, we should sue that pound, deceiving us like that. This dog will be a monster and now we are stuck with her. Betsy never did things like this." Of course daddy defended me, "She is just a puppy, she will learn. Remember how destructive Betsy was, at least this one is not."

Mom said, "I give her credit for that, take her directly to the bathroom and give her a bath." Oh no, another bath. That was punishment enough for me, so I learned my lesson not to do that again.

Mom always talks about Betsy. Betsy did this, and Betsy did that. In a way it is good hearing it, and I am trying hard to be like her. Like Betsy, I now poop and pee on one side of the house, and never make a mess on the carpet or in he car, and never touch Mommy's yarn, plants, and knick-knacks. If they are pretending to hit each other, I cover the one being hit with my body. I fetch the ball at least four times before I hint to them to get it themselves. I do not eat their food.

I know the rule. The food on the coffee table is theirs, on the floor mine. Mommy always tests me. She will deliberately leave the food on the table to see if I will eat it. It would be very easy to do, since I am now a whole lot taller than the table, but I never do. I want to show her I am just like Betsy, if not better. She doesn't complain anymore, there is practically nothing to complain about except my shedding and whining. Well I can't do anything about my shedding. As for whining, it gets me what I want so I don't think I will drop it either; she will just have to live with it. I have these two wrapped around my paws, and there is one thing I can do that Betsy can't. I can put my big paws around my mom. She always gets a kick out of it. "Oh, she is hugging me," she would say. I do not think she still thinks of me as retarded, since I have learned all Betsy's habits without them teaching or telling me. I just learned it from listening to their conversations. Now tell me, if I am not smart!

As I look at her pounding on the keyboard, writing about Betsy, I can't help but ask myself, "Do I have to wait seventeen years for her to write about me?"

A true animal story written for young family members

Brandy's Rabbit

Jim Laird

Many years ago on a warm winter day, my wife and I went for a walk around our property in the Sierra foothills; our Springer spaniel pup "Brandy" joined us. She was dancing around us exploring the sides of the driveway as we walked out to our dirt road, never getting very far away. We had gone about 200 feet along the road when Brandy left our side and dashed into the brush. She started barking and looking back at us, then down at the ground in front of her. I could just see her through the bushes and nothing else. I was not about to crawl through the brush to see what she was excited about, so we just kept walking. When she did not join us, I started calling her. We had gone quite a way before she stopped barking and joined us.

About an hour later, we completed our walk and were again at the entrance of our driveway. Recognizing the area, Brandy ran back to the spot where she had been barking when we started our walk and began barking. My curiosity was aroused; I bent down close to the ground and forced my way through the brush and down on my knees to get near her. She looked up at me excitedly with those soft brown eyes saying; "look what I found" There lay a baby rabbit still in its birth sack. Picking it up, I found it was still alive, but getting cold. Clearing away the sack, I dried it off with my shirttail. Placing it in my shirt pocket to keep warm we returned home. I made a nest for it with some rags and placed it on top of the water heater for warmth. When I returned a little later it was gone. Looking behind the water heater, I found it on the floor between the heater and dryer. The little newborn was still alive and covered in lint. Wiping off the lint, I placed it in a shoebox and put it back on the water heater. On my next check the little guy was perky and alert.

We hunted up an eyedropper and got him to take a few drops of warm milk. A couple days later, I called the vet for information on proper care for the bunny, as he was doing great.

The vet said; add Karo syrup to canned milk. That did the trick. We called Brandy's rabbit "Peter" and he did well and became a great pet. House training was not his best virtue. Peter often climbed on my lap to sleep and up the back of my chair where he would nibble my ear or hop onto the windowsill to watch the world go by.

His food went to fresh veggies and rabbit food as he got older. We made a pen with out a bottom and often put him outside where he could eat fresh grass. I would move it around to new areas as needed.

Now he had the long ears and back legs of a Jackrabbit. When he seemed ready to return to the wild, we turned him loose near our spring with his box and rabbit food. For the next couple years we would often see a rabbit standing along our road that did not run off when we drove by. We are sure it was Brandy's rabbit.

Escapade

Ariel Edmundson

Stop that prancing Satyr
Goat let go!
Desire is satiated
Our garland of flowers dead.
We sang to the pipes of Pan
Drank wine, danced at Bacchus side.
We were lost in Paradise
Reality found us and we returned.
Our Arcadia is no more
Singing and dancing no more.
The music has ended
Fires of passion flame,
Smoldered and died
All desire stamped out
Like a pressed grape souring
rotting in the sun.

The class assignment was to write a story about food.

Burnt Toast

Luther Mandell

Burning toast is a modern version of a cooking disaster that dates back to ancient times. Long, long ago when cooks didn't have temperature gauges nor clock settings to guide their cooking, such as 20 minutes at 350 degrees per pound of turkey, cooking was hit or miss. When it is overdone, especially meat, food gets really tough and dry, and isn't fit for human consumption. Still, one doesn't pick up a mastodon steak at the local hunting grounds every day.

Food didn't get thrown out because it was overdone, not fit to eat; yet not to get thrown out was a complete waste. Today we would give it to the dogs. But the religious leaders of that day said "give it to the gods."

The epicurean disaster of that day became a burnt offering. There was a reason so much food was offered to the gods. It wasn't that the people were overly religious. Rather from the interpretations of tablets recently found a department of food and nutrition of that day kept harping on the dangers of eating undercooked meat. People took it to heart, went overboard, hence the ready supply of burnt offerings.

My Aunt Tillie followed the advice of that ancient department of food and nutrition. Remember when you were a child the constant admonition to chew before swallowing? When my Aunt Tillie cooked meat, she not only sealed in the juices, she extracted them. You not only chewed the food, you masticated it. It became a contest to see if you could tenderize it by chewing before you got tired of it all and swallowed.

Just remember, if you burn the toast, don't scrape off the burnt portion, follow tradition. Give it to the church!

Awakening to the Beauty and Sounds of Early Morning

Early Morning Light

Carol Jean Main

How thrilling to me are the colors - of early morning light.
The soft grayed hues - of greens and blues - so bright.
Where the sun peeps through - only here and there,
While I stand at the window breathing in sweet air.
So clear and cool - while the sounds travel far,
The whistle of the milk train - the wheels of a car.
A bird calls "We're hungry" - to its little mate,
The babies are peeping - it's getting late.
The grass has the sparkle of early morning dew,
A refreshing bath - to begin day anew.
How precious to me - for so quickly they pass,
The soft colors - the cool air - the dew on the grass.
How in a twinkling of an eye - the day is here,
as warmth fills the air on this great hemisphere.
Now - the sun will prevail - forever, it seems,
while the morn slowly passes, as if in a dream.

This story is meant for those that fret over jury duty.

Jury Duty

Dick Cory

 My jury summons is for April 9, 2003, at 8:00 a.m. Since I'm semi-retired there is no problem with this Superior Court call. Why is it that I so dread these notices? Am I the only potential juror who harbors these thoughts? I think not.
 To compound my anxiety, a recorded message from the court last evening said that my group number, 316, had been postponed until 1:00 p.m. Now the tension builds as this is compromising my writing class time. Now *"they"* are interrupting my retirement plan. I would feel differently if I were being dismissed from work for jury duty, but retirement time for which I've worked so hard, no way!
 I dream-up excuses for not serving the courts as I travel to the county seat. Some I have heard from others, and some are my creation. Attire is most important. Look the opposite of what a lawyer wants and you are home free. The stereotypes of redneck, hippie, punk rocker, liberal, conservative, alcoholic, radical ethicist all come to mind.
 A friend of mine says that he selects radical publications for the lawyers to see him reading. Examples might include the *National Riflemen Association Journal, Penthouse, The Oklahoma Observer* or a Michael Moore's book. Of course the clothing must match the reading material.
 But what real excuses do I have? Would my answer: "Would you please repeat that question," to every question give the judge and lawyers a clue? Maybe if I turned my hearing aid volume controls either up or down, would that help?
 Does being diabetic count for anything? I guess not. It doesn't cause my refusal of membership in a health club. I don't want to chance losing my driver's license by claiming poor eyesight. What else can I think up?

As I get closer to the Courthouse, my conscience begins to gnaw on me. Am I unpatriotic for not wanting to serve? After all isn't it my civic duty to answer the call of the courts? What makes me think that I should be disqualified before someone else? Wait a minute, who's on trial here anyway?

Going through the security gate, these counter thoughts are racing through my brain. Will anyone detect my desire to escape from this duty?

I notice an unusual number of people carrying babies in car seats. Each seat is checked for weapons, but I know why these crying kids are there. This is a scam that I hadn't thought of. You think one of these parents would loan her baby to me just for the selection process. No way would they relinquish this jury dismissal reason.

Is it the tedium of the uncertainty of long waits that discourages me? Could it be the responsibility of passing judgment on the fate of an accused? Why do I try so hard to avoid what I would appreciate others doing for me? Be still oh conscience.

As I walk down the hallway, I am dreading the solitary confinement of hours spent waiting in straight back chairs, while lawyers and a judge conjure up questions to ask me. Will I perjure myself in my attempt to escape this "sentence"? There must be others that really want to experience jury duty. I hope they go easy on me.

I hand my jury summons to the clerk stationed behind the opening in the thick window. She scans it three times and reads my record on a computer screen. She gives it back telling me that I'm excused for another year. My group has been dismissed. My trial of nerves has ended. A smile creeps over my face, knowing that justice has been served.

This poem questions if there will ever be really good poetry to come from my pen. Perhaps the words will stay hidden forever in my wishful heart.

Sifting

Roger E. Honzik

I sift the dusty tailings
Of the thoughts within my mind
For a clear and gentle rhythm
To the feelings left behind.

Ever just eluding
As they weave their patterns free
Then unravel in the instant
I would write to have them be.

Will I ever gain the focus
To present my rhymes one day
Or am I to be their keeper
Lacking words my thoughts to say.

I will sift and ever listen
As my heart weaves tender themes
That one day may surface softly
Adding voice to hidden dreams.

This is about a challenge I was forced to take that could have been a matter of life or death, for one of us.

Remembering and Wondering Why?

Richard A. Main

It was a pretty drive up into the canyon and when we reached the end, we parked and got out and walked up the stream. We had noticed that the restaurant was closed but wanting to make the most of our trip, a walk seemed a good idea at the time. About a block up the stream, Carol decided to take off her shoes and wade. My wife is crazy about water, I could take it or leave it.

I sat on a rock and we enjoyed the time there. All of a sudden we heard loud talking and laughing and three girls appeared on the path. One girl was quite large and tall. She wore a scanty sundress and high heeled sandals and they carried coke bottles. After they went on past us, Carol remarked that an outfit like that wasn't very sensible for such an outing. "High heels on a rocky path is just plain dumb" she remarked with disgust. I agreed.

A few minutes later we heard a scream and glass breaking - then "Help!"

Carol said "Go!" and I did as she quickly put on her shoes on wet feet and followed me.

The big girl lay on the ground, her leg in a twisted position and she was sobbing loudly. The broken coke bottle lay on the ground beside her. Her bare back and shoulders exposed to the rocks and dirt. Her leg had to be broken.

The other girls were crying softly and seemed helpless in the situation. I told Carol to stay with her, and I went off to the truck to get an army blanket we always carried with us. I planned to find a phone and call for help. When I reached the truck and got the blanket, there were three young men near by, looking curiously at me.

I told them what had happened and asked them to find a phone and call for an ambulance as there was no phone on the outside of the closed restaurant. They promised they would stop at the first phone.

I had done all I could and went back to the girl. Carol helped me put the blanket under her and partly covered her up with it. The wounded girl was crying uncontrollably. I felt sorry for her but felt anger that she had got herself in such a mess.

Now we, too, were involved and far more than I, at that moment, realized. Doing what I had to do was probably the toughest thing I ever did in my life.

It seemed hours before the ambulance arrived. We heard the siren and I ran back to meet it. When the two women got out, I just couldn't believe what I saw. They sent women paramedics! It was then, I knew we were in for trouble.

They took out the gurney and followed me up the narrow path, full of trees. We had to practically squeeze past some of them. There was just no way they could carry that gurney with that heavy girl who weighed close to 300 pounds, up the narrow trail. They soon realized it too, but, after lifting her on it, with all of our help, one paramedic came up with the only solution.

"We will just have to carry her down stream." So the two women, who weren't that big, took up one end, I was told to lift up the other. With all the strength I could muster, I lifted her, feeling my head would burst.

The women led the way, leaving me in back. As we waded into the stream, my feet hit rocks, slippery and hidden in the water, for I couldn't see where I was going. The gurney was in front of me. The women could see in front of them for the gurney was in back of them. When they started off too fast, I yelled to slow down, that I couldn't see where I was going.

They realized my problem and took it slow, but still not slow enough, for I had to stop with every step and feel for the next foothold. I could see me, slipping, with the girl on top of me, in the water. I'd have broken bones for sure. So, we crept on, stopping and starting, the girl sobbing all the while. I too, wanted to sob. But it took all my strength to keep going.

Carol was keeping up with us on the trail, constantly saying; "Be careful!"

We finally made it to the parking lot and up to the ambulance. By then, no way could I lift her up into it. My wet shoes sloshed with each step. I felt cuts and bruises on my feet and said a silent prayer, a minute later a car drove up and a man got out. He had the strength to make the final lift. So, with the girl on her way to the hospital, I got into our car and collapsed for a while. But hungry by then, I finally got up the steam to go back to Whiskeytown and find some food. After a meal, I felt strong enough to start home.

On the way back down, we stopped at the dam and went into the visitor's lookout room to use their restroom. We told the person on duty about our escapade. She warned me I had better be checked, saying I didn't look good. I knew that! I'd seen myself in the mirror. My face was pale. I looked beat!

Carol had never driven our truck and was hesitant to try so I forced myself to keep going. We did make it home, by stopping several times to rest.

Next day, I saw a doctor and he discovered a heart murmur, something I had never had. In time it did seem to disappear, but left me with a worry that I could face a heart problem someday. But, now, they say I'm OK. Time healed my heart.

One year after settling down in Paradise, California, I awoke to discover snow was falling and had been doing so long enough to cover the ground. When we looked around for the place to retire, it appeared that Paradise would be snowless. Actually I was pleased, it was close to Christmas.

Snow ... Maybe

Alison K. Paolini

It doesn't snow in Paradise!
Well then, tell me if you will,
What is that white stuff covering the ground?
The pine cones are bedecked in ermine,
While the squirrel scatters something
With each twitch of his tail.

Oh, but it doesn't snow, well almost never, hardly ever.
How could it have snowed in Paradise?
I know I was told emphatically that the climate was mild,
Tho rain became a bore late in winter and sometimes froze.
But it doesn't snow .. no it won't .. it certainly seldom does.

Today I rose in the early hours to the quiet we know
as snow ...
Later, I saw a small flurry of cotton fall off a twig, loosened
by a breeze.
Still later, I felt the cold in my hand, as I rolled that stuff
into a ball.

And yes .. of course ..though it couldn't be snow ..
I rolled it tight and hard.
I took solid aim and with all my might
Threw that non-snowball across the yard.

Since I was nine years old, I have wondered if I am genetically connected with those who raised me.

The Veil

Delores Swenson Squyres

Who am I? This is a problem I have pondered ever since my mother's funeral when I was nine years old. I happened to be standing nearby when I heard the minister ask my grandfather if he could see the family Bible. My grandfather took him into the living room, then placed the Bible on the library table, and opened it to a leaf in the front of the Bible. The minister looked at it, and then left. As soon as they both were gone, I sidled up to it, and looked at the list. What were they looking for? I quickly realized it was a list of all of the grandchildren, starting with my brother, and continuing in the order of their birth. Suddenly, I received a great shock! All of those born before me were listed, and all born after me, but my name was not on the list!

The first opportunity I had, I asked my grandfather why my name was not on that list. He turned his back to me and walked away. I was shocked! Before that my grandfather had always answered any question I asked him. If he didn't know the answer, he told me so. Why did he refuse to tell me this time?

Just a little later I heard my aunts and the minister discussing me again. This time it was about whether or not I had been baptized in the church. The minister said there was no record of it. My aunts started arguing. The one aunt insisted that the minister had been drunk when he baptized me, and so he didn't write it in the records. Another said that it had never happened. However, after a look from the first aunt, the second was silent. The third aunt remained silent. The minister looked at them, but said nothing. So now I had another thing to wonder about.

One day I overheard my grandmother and aunt talking. They had been talking about me. But now they were talking about a baby being born with a veil over its eyes, and how sad that was.

What did that mean? Was that me they were talking about? Is there something bad connected with it and I was that baby? Why didn't I ask? How I wish I had!

When I started working and could pay for it, I sent for a copy of my birth certificate. It said I was born at Willmar Hospital, Kandiyohi County, Minnesota, listed my parents names, and the name of the doctor. It also listed that I was legitimate. But when it came to my name, it said Baby as a first name, Girl as a second name. I have often wondered why. My brother's name was on his birth certificate.

When Social Security started, my grandmother had to go to the Social Security Office and swear that I was the person referred to on that birth record. They called me, to ask how to spell my name they actually had my grandmother talk to me and ask. I hadn't even thought about it. The family had not known how to spell it, so I spelled it however I wanted. Now I was asked for an immediate answer. So I spelled it as the Mexicans did ----Dolores, but I knew that wasn't correct. My grandmother also said it wasn't correct, but that's how the Social Security people spelled it, and that was that. They demanded that I return the copy of the birth certificate I had, or I would not be given a Social Security number. They sent me a new birth certificate, different from the original.

In recent years, my oldest daughter found a baby picture postcard of me, and there, in my mother's handwriting, was the name spelled "delouris". My grandmother had told me that my mother had been reading a French novel when she was pregnant and the heroine in that story was named "delouris".

For three years I worked on the genealogy of my maternal grandparents, and some on my paternal grandparents. I worked diligently, with much assistance from Suzanne Brown and others at the Family History center. I spent what available money I had renting films through them from the Mormon Center in Utah. In some instances, I had followed these families back to the early seventeen hundreds. Then, one day I asked myself, "Why are you doing this? Why are you spending all your time and money, and you aren't even certain that this is your family." So I stopped. That brought up the old question, who am I?

So, here I am, eighty-eight years old.
And I still do not know who I am.

Being all alone on my honeymoon had not been my dream, nor was the danger I faced when my life was threatened.

Death Stalked the Kern

Carol Jean Main

Here I am, all alone, in our long awaited honeymoon cottage on the Kern River. This was not how we had planned it since our wedding, six months before. Nor did we know when we rented the cottage that 'death' stalked the river.

Excitement had been building as I happily packed. A well-stocked ice chest was ready. We would be quite a distance from town, so I was going prepared. Isolation was what we wanted and we were getting it. Just time together, fishing, swimming and hiking had been our dream, but dreams don't always come true.

Fate intervened. When Mark drove in, he was slow coming in. "Why doesn't he hurry?" I wondered? My heart skipped a beat when I finally saw his face.

"Hon - I honestly don't know how to tell you this..."

"Mark - what is it?" I was getting frantic.

"My boss is sick with the flu. I can't leave yet." He spoke almost defiantly, as though he thought I'd protest and blame him.
Instead - I broke into tears. We'd saved for this. To get the cabin, we had paid in advance - no refund.

Cabins to rent this late in the season were impossible. School was starting and most people closed down this late in the year.

I had noticed a redheaded woman sunbathing on their deck next door, and made a mental note not to be overly friendly. We wanted to be alone. I dried my tears as an idea hit me.

"Sweetheart - you can't help it, and I'm disappointed, but flu doesn't last long. I'm sure your boss will be back to work in a day or so. Since I'm all packed, why don't we go up tonight as planned? I'll stay and you return home early in the morning to work. We're just lucky we live in Bakersfield, near enough to do this.

"But Honey, you'd be so alone there with no car or phone."

"Yes, but there are people next door. I saw a woman sunbathing. I'll get acquainted with her and I'm sure she would help me if I need it. I'll be just fine."

"Well, if you're sure you won't be afraid or nervous?"

"Who, me? You know I'm a brave woman. Remember you married a W.A.C."

"Oh yes, I'd nearly forgotten that little fact." Smiling, he kissed me.

We ate our supper in silence each busy with our own thoughts. I was already alone in the cabin wishing Mark were there with me.

He, no doubt, was alone in our house missing me. We were in love!

Our ride up the mountain seemed endless. I was concerned for Mark having to go back down so soon. "Surely, this is the right thing to do?" I murmured.

"If you are worrying about my part in it missing you will be the hardest. And I'll eat my meals out, since you've got all the food." He laughed then.

"Yes, Darling, and no doubt most of the fresh food will spoil. My appetite will leave with you. But I'll relax and swim. Probably take a walk."

"Hey, Hon, that could be dangerous. Please don't do those things alone. Wait for me!" He said, imploringly.

"Mark, I'll be careful. You know I'm a strong swimmer and the river is way down. Remember - it's the end of summer. I'll just wade and get wet to cool off during the heat of the day. Besides, I'm sure I'll be swimming with my new friend from next door." I smiled recalling my earlier thought how I'd play it cool. Little did I know how cool!

The cabin was dark and cold when we arrived. But Mark got a fire going in the wood stove while I put away our things.

"This is fun!" I exclaimed. Then, we both made up the bed and got ready to retire.

"Honey, come out here. Look at that sky." I walked over and stood beside him. He pulled me close as we gazed at the moon shining on the water. "What a perfect setting!" We both said at once. From then on, we didn't waste words - but our romantic interlude came to a sudden halt when I felt Mark stiffen and squeeze my arm.

"Quick inside!" While he pulled me with him through the door, He yanked at the drapes to close them.

"Mark, what on earth was that all about?" I demanded.

"Susan." He never called me this unless it was a serious matter. "I heard a noise in the bushes. It probably was an animal." I felt a chilling sensation. We waited for something we knew not what? When nothing happened we relaxed and discussed the situation. "Mark, it was probably a deer." I wanted very much to believe this.
"Honey, you are probably right. I guess my imagination got spooked. Didn't know I was such a coward." He grinned.
"Well, I promise you one thing, I won't go out there alone at night while you're gone. Animal or no animal!"
"No! Or anywhere else alone. Please stay put here at the cabin. Otherwise, I won't leave, job or no job."
"Mark, don't be ridiculous! You must go and I will be good, I promise. Guess I'm not quite as brave as I thought I was."
"O.K. Sweetheart, now let's go to bed. I'm tired enough to sleep even in a strange bed," and we both did. The alarm was set for five o'clock. It arrived too fast.

With coffee and oatmeal inside of him, Mark kissed me goodbye, with a last offer to take me with him. But I declined. I went back to bed; however, my sleepiness had left when Mark did. So I just lay there and thought how I'd start my day,

With dishes done and the bed made, I dressed and picked up a writing tablet and pen. On the deck, I settled down in a comfortable chaise lounge. My correspondence had suffered lately. I'd catch up.

Time escaped me. I was really enjoying myself. The mountain air was so wonderful and the river lapped along, bubbling and gurgling like only a river can. It was all so restful that I dozed. How long I slept I didn't know, but I awoke with a start. The sun was hot on my back and I was terribly thirsty.

Was that why I awakened? I seemed to have heard something. Oh, well, no big deal. It may have been a bird, I told myself, and got up and went into the house.

It was very dark after the outside glare. I got a cool drink and turned around and gasped. The front door was ajar. Surely I'd locked it? But it was unlocked. Maybe I didn't quite close it after forgetting to lock it? Well, it was possible. I was probably half asleep when Mark left.

The latch clicking open must have been what awakened me. A breeze could have blown it open. This time I securely locked it. Feeling a little hungry, I made a ham sandwich and a cup of tea and sat at the window overlooking the river.

After a short nap on the bed, I got up and looked out.

"Oh baloney!" I exclaimed to nobody.

"I want to go swimming. After all, I'm a good swimmer and I will be sensible. Mark is being foolishly protective."

I broke my promise to him and donned my swimsuit, my more modest one. Pinning my door key to the inside of my bra, I went down the path to the river.

The water was warm and wonderful on my skin. The current wasn't too strong. I began swimming, just far enough out to stay up. The water was bubbly and so relaxing; I just floated awhile with my head up to see where I was going. Ahead, a large fallen tree was sticking up out of the water and the river separated there, dividing into two channels.

I decided that if I kept to the bank side, I'd avoid the danger area. When I reached the tree, I got out on the bank and went back up stream. This was great fun! I did this several times until I tired myself.

Suddenly remembering Mark's warning not to go off alone, I decided against the temptation to dry off on the sandy beach. Instead, I went back to the cabin's deck and stretched out on the chaise lounge. Though still alone, I was at least at home base.

Once more, I went to sleep and a cool breeze awakened me. Feeling chilled, I went around the house to the front door and used my key. The door had stayed locked this time, to my relief.

After a hot shower, I was hungry now and thinking of what to fix. A meat patty and potato salad brought from home inside me, I grew restless and decided to take a short walk. Perhaps the neighbors would be out and I'd get acquainted. But all was quiet next door.

Remembering my promise, I only went a short distance instead of the long walk I was wanting. Returning, I sat on the deck again for awhile, glancing at a magazine but mostly just enjoying the view and wonderful air. Then, as it grew darker, I remembered our first night there and quickly drew the drapes about the same speed as Mark had"Brave me!" I mused, feeling a slight chilling sensation.

With nothing better to do, I went to bed and listened to the radio. Loneliness was overtaking me, I was missing Mark and wondering what he was doing. I was also having some regrets and an eerie feeling made me get up and check the doors and windows. All were locked. Sleep finally got the better of me.

Next day, I wrote more letters and went swimming again. Still no sight or sound from next door. "Perhaps they've gone?" Then I wished I'd checked for lights the night before. But as I passed the front of their cabin, I looked up in time to catch a movement at their window. With a sigh of relief that they were still there, I waded into the water and swam. "Maybe they'll join me." I thought, longingly. But after swimming several times, down to the tree, I was on my last lap before giving up. I was almost to the tree again, my right arm raised in a stroke, when something very heavy hit it and I sank under the surface, stunned. Then I rose up, sputtering, my eyes all blurred, I saw a dark figure hurrying up the bank above me. Silhouetted against the afternoon sun, I wasn't sure if it was a man or woman.

With my heart pounding and my arm throbbing I had to get out of sight quick. Whoever it was had been aiming at my head. "I must get behind the tree and hide!" I decided. Swimming underwater, I kept my eyes open so I wouldn't run into the tree. Then I saw it. There was my redheaded neighbor, tied to a limb under water. Quite dead! Now I knew why my life had been threatened. I was getting too close to her and would become a danger to her killer.

My lungs were nearly bursting. I came up for air, feeling my heart had stopped beating. I gasped and choked, praying he hadn't seen me or heard me, that he believed I had drowned. Creeping farther from the body, I waited until darkness gave me cover to crawl out of the water. Swimming quickly over her body, I was shaking and chilled to the bone as I made my way along the beach.

The moon went behind a cloud as I went cautiously up to the cabin and crept around to the front. But as my foot hit the step to go up, I was grabbed from behind. My screams drowned out my name. "Susan!" Mark hollered the second time before I heard him I fainted in his arms.

Then he realized that I was only in a wet swimsuit. He'd worried about me so much that he drove up after work. Angrily, he shook me to bring me around.

Then it was my turn to tell him all I'd been through. Hugging me to him, he cried, "Oh, My God!"

"Yes, Mark." I cried back. "I prayed to have you come, and you came, even if you did scare me half to death! I needed you." As we clung together, I whispered a thankful prayer and so did Mark. We grew closer at that moment

Then I said, "Darling, don't ever trust me to be brave again."

"Never!" He answered

That man next door was finally apprehended. He'd already gone home and reported his wife had left with her lover. "She can stay away, as far as I'm concerned!" He'd said, angrily. My appearance and report changed the picture for him.

Being at the end of summer, he felt safe that her body wouldn't be discovered. Winter storms would destroy all evidence. Then, I'd become a threat to him, I was to die also, being found down river, one day, with a bump on the head, but certainly no proof of murder.

The landlady gave us credit on the cabin. With Mark beside me, I can face the Kern River again. But I will never forget how 'death' had stalked it.

Who is Behind This Great Force?

Awareness!

Carol Jean Main

How jade green is the rolling sea today,
The storm is off, but not far away.
Great waves come in to crash on the shore,
We stroll on the sand in safety no more.
For soon those waves will reach inland,
As now, the bluffs in water stand.
The roar is deafening as the waves pound the sand,
Now gone is that sight of beach and the land.
Except for those bluffs that appear to float,
Like a giant ship with its' skipper remote.
The eucalyptus trees in the distance sway,
Like a great silver sail off faraway.
The clouds billow out then darkness prevails,
Along comes rain then wind then hail.
The fierce storm is a flying force,
Frightening and wild it is on course.
As we watch the heavens opening wide,
And see the results of the incoming tide,
We become so aware who's behind this great force,
Realizing what's in store, if we sail off our course.

This poem paints some of the sad realities of the inner city, cold and uncaring before dawn.

The East End of Night

Roger E. Honzik

Breezes push
The stale and sooty smells of night,

As a lamppost maiden
drags her pain to the mission's door
with its faded rays of hope.

Cold within his pasteboard box
a sockless derelict curls,
his half drained bottle waits.

A hungry yellow cat
moves past.

Chill this time
before the dawn,
as child starts to cry.

"Mamma, I fall down"
"Mother, Stephanie is going to Joan's house after church and they never even invited me."
"Oh, Mom, Tom wants a divorce."
"Baby, Mother will kiss it and make it all better."

In Retrospect

Dawn McFarland

She came to me at almost three
with her broken doll and skinned up knee,
and mamma kissed and held her tight,
until everything again was right
in her little world of nearly three.

She came again when she was ten,
to share a hurt dealt by her friend,
Mother held her so very tight
'til everything again was right -
It takes longer, though, at the age of ten.

Today, as she nears three times ten
the pain is worse than it was then.
I long to hold her oh so tight
And tell her everything will be alright,
but she's reluctant to believe that line
now that she is twenty-nine.

The Vase

Beverly Strisower

It was winter in Michigan. I was with the debate team from our high school. We had just completed a debate against another team from, perhaps, Dearborn.
I don't remember if we won or lost.
We had to wait for some time for the parents to return to collect us for the thirty-mile trip back to Ypsilanti, our hometown.
Rather than wait in the cold of that winter day, we filled the time by exploring the stores near the host high school. One store was a small 5&10. A boy from our debate team was with me. We walked up and down the aisles of the store, checking out the merchandise. Just looking, not planning to buy.
And then, there it was. A tiny white vase with a classical shape, just big enough for one pansy blossom. Just big enough to put in the palm of my hand. It cost 10 cents. The boy was there beside me; he said, "Just take it. Nobody will miss it." I couldn't do it.
We walked around the store some more and returned to the counter where the little vase waited. This time, I looked around.
No one was in sight. I took the little vase and put it in my pocket. We looked around some more and then casually left the store.

On the ride home, my conscience began to hurt. I squirmed in discomfort. The little vase in my pocket was a hard lump against my hip.

When I got home, I put the tiny vase in the farthest recesses of my closet, out of sight. But not out of mind.

I graduated from high school and went to college. When I moved from home to my first job in Yale, Michigan, the little white vase was still in my closet.

Still a reproach.

I packed my books and my clothes. And then I took the little white vase and carefully wrapped it in waste paper and put it in the garbage can.

The years have come and gone. The memory of that tiny vase is still a potent deterrent. I have never again been tempted to steal anything under any circumstance.

A Little Bird's Tale

Beverly Strisower

This story begins a year ago on a warm, sunny day. I was out in the garden, quietly and slowly inspecting the flowerbeds for damage done by the winter winds and rains. I became aware of a small flash of yellow on the back fence. This bit of yellow moved from one place on top of the fence to another. As I looked more closely, this proved to be a little golden parakeet. I knew immediately that the little bird was lost. I talked quietly to the little yellow bird as I very slowly advanced toward the fence. I put out my finger for the little bird to come to me. The little bird hopped from one side of my outstretched hand to the other. It was not afraid but it didn't like the idea of getting on my finger. I kept talking and reassuring the little bird. Finally, when it seemed that we were at an impasse, I turned slowly to leave. Without hesitation, the little bird flew to my shoulder. I continued to talk to it as I moved slowly toward the house. My thought was to get the little bird inside where it would be safe and then work out some housing for it.

The little bird rode on my shoulder into the house. Now it was safe. We went through the kitchen and into the garage. I was able to get a spare cage and bring it back into the kitchen. The little bird was still on my shoulder. I filled the feeder in the black cage with bird food and birdseed. I put fresh water in the water dish. The little bird hopped onto the top of the cage and then slid down the bars of the cage to the open door. The little bird looked around a bit and then sank onto one of the perches in the cage. It seemed very tired. I moved away from the cage and continued to watch from a distance.

More than an hour went by. Finally, the little bird began to explore this new place. It found the food and water and began to eat, tentatively at first and then eagerly.

Obviously this little bird must have been lost recently. Its yellow feathers glistened with good health; not a feather was out of place. How could I find the owner?

I got the morning paper and looked in the want ads for pets. One person had an ad for a lost parakeet. I called. A cultured voice answered. The woman said that her parakeet was yellow. The woman asked if she could come to see the bird as soon as possible. I gave her my address.

A few minutes later, a nicely dressed woman with a stylish blond hairdo arrived. She carried a well cared-for cage in one hand; in the other she held a large flowering plant. She said, "This is for you. May I see the bird you found?" I thanked her for the flowers as I showed her to the kitchen and the black cage with the little yellow bird. She looked carefully. The little bird looked back with little interest. The woman said sadly, "He's prettier than my Buddy. He's not my bird. If you can't find this little bird's owner, would you let me know? I would be happy to take him." I promised that I would let her know what was happening. She gave me her address and phone number. As she left, I said, "I'll let you know."

Now what should I do? Try the local paper, I guess. I was pleased to hear that the paper publishes ads for lost pets without charge. What a good thing to do for lost animals! The ad taker and I agree on the wording of an ad for the next day's paper. "Are there any other places where people report lost pets?" I ask. The ad taker tells me that the local SPCA sometimes gets calls about lost pets. I thank her for her help.

When I call the SPCA, the person who answered said she would check on any reports of lost birds. I wait on the line. She tells me that there is one report about a yellow parakeet, which has been lost for two weeks. We agree that this seems unlikely to be the same bird as the little one I had found. She gives me the phone number to call anyway. I promise to call to check.

I dial the number. After some rings, the phone is answered. I explain that I have found a little yellow parakeet and the SPCA has given me his number. The man says, "It's my kid's bird. She got it for her birthday last year. This year, at her birthday party, the bird escaped."

I ask, "When could you come and see if this is your bird?"

He answers, "Can't come now. I'm resting. I'll come over about five this afternoon."

Late in the afternoon, there are several emphatic bangs on the front door. I open the door to see a scruffy, poorly dressed, bearded man and a little girl dressed in very worn clothes. The little girl carries a battered cage. "Can I see if it's Pretty?" asks the little girl. I lead her into the kitchen. Her father tags behind. As soon as the little girl gets into the kitchen the little bird begins to hop excitedly from one side of the cage to the other. The little girl goes quietly to the cage and talks softly to the little bird. She opens the cage door and Pretty flies to her shoulder. She says "Pretty doesn't like fingers, he likes shoulders." They stand nose to beak and chirp and chuckle to each other. Both are delighted to have found each other again. We marvel that this little yellow bird has been able to stay alive for more than two weeks in a neighborhood full of cats and at least one hawk. During this time the little bird has flown several blocks from the little girl's home to mine.

The father says, "We best be gittin' home." The little girl puts Pretty in his cage and closes the door. She gives me a look full of warmth and gratitude as she carries her bird out the front door. The father's back retreats without a word.

I call the stylish blond woman and tell her that the little yellow bird has been claimed. I tell her the circumstances.

I clean the black cage and put it back into the garage – until next time.

Acknowledgements

The generosity of businesses, organizations
and individuals made this project possible

Hannie J. Voyles
Creative Writing - Personal History
Editor/Advisor
Group Travel Advisor/Director
530-342-9041

Roger Honzik
Marion Williams
Mr. and Mrs. Russ Biederman
Dina D. Kinnune
Norma Hill
M.C. Madelyn Trust
L. & M. Daroczi
Ariel Edmundson
Millie Steele
James Laird
Darlene Fuentes
Gary A. Incaudo, M.D.
Sally Wallis
Carol Bingman Nielson
Janice Nelson
Dolores Squyres
Carmen and Robert Jury
Shirley Smith
Margaret Hughes
Alice M. Duncan

Health and Care
Facility
855 Bruce Rd
Chico, Ca 95928
530-566-1800

FinancialNetwork
530.342.2900
800.333.2901
Fax 530.342.3925

Anne Johnson
Financial Consultant

2452 Lakewest Drive, Chico, CA 95928
johnsona@financialnetwork.com - CA Ins. Lic. #0C50414

Art Campion
STORE MANAGER
NORTHERN CALIFORNIA DIVISION

1016 W SACRAMENTO AVE
CHICO, CA 95926
PHONE (530) 895-0244
FAX (530) 895-1507

Bill and Barbara Allen
Supporters
Paradise, CA.

Josh Frantz - Advanced Hearing
Instruments
Chico, CA
530-893-HEAR (4327)

Ed and Sigrida Vidners
Foothill Carpet Cleaning
Chico 530-345-1003
Paradise 530-872-2403

Stevyn Voyles-Menegazzi
Progressive Physical Therapy
406-249-0209

TACO BELL
Oroville, CA

Chico Optical Lab
Expert handling of optical devices,
and prescriptions
530-895-1474

Ronald B. Morrow
Financial Consultant
213-452-2117

Robert Clark DDS
Rio Lindo Dental Associates
Chico, CA

Autographs

ISBN 1-41204666-1